BUILDING WITH BAMBOO

Building with Bamboo

A handbook

Second edition

DR JULES J. A. JANSSEN

INTERMEDIATE TECHNOLOGY PUBLICATIONS

Intermediate Technology Publications Limited,
103-105 Southampton Row, London WC1B 4HH, UK

© Intermediate Technology Publications 1995

Reprinted 1999

A CIP record for this book is available from the British Library
ISBN 1 85339 203 0

Typesetting by Diamond People, Bromyard
Printed by SRP, Exeter

Contents

Preface

In May 1974 a manual on bamboo was published in Dutch. This manual contained selected articles on the experiences of Dutch engineers in Indonesia many years ago, with the building of houses, roads and bridges. Since these articles had a wealth of practical information, they were considered to be still useful for fieldworkers.

After publication, several requests for an English translation were received and, instead of translating the Dutch text, similar original English material was brought together in 1979, resulting in a manual for use by field engineers and community development workers in tropical countries. In 1982 these manuals were enlarged with the results of modern research programmes.

In 1987 it was felt that these manuals should be replaced by a new handbook, giving useful information on building with bamboo. This handbook was intended for those who have to build (or even like to build) with bamboo.

This manual has now been revised, with some new information reflecting the latest knowledge of building with bamboo, and the addition of a case study from Costa Rica.

Some presuppositions with this book are that:

o   the reader has some basic technical knowledge about building;

o   the reader works in a developing country;

o   bamboo occurs in the region concerned;

o   the use of foreign currency should be avoided.

The author hopes that this handbook might help many people to solve their problems.

JULES JANSSEN

Eindhoven, The Netherlands

November 1994

1. Introduction

There are about 600 different botanical species of bamboo in the world, and each of them is characterized by properties peculiar to itself. The close observer will find that in each bamboo-using community certain species of bamboo will be used for certain purposes. This handbook shows what opportunities there are of using local bamboos to meet local needs.

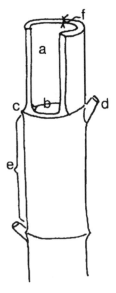

Figure 1.1: The parts of a bamboo

a. Cavity
b. Diaphragm
c. Node
d. Branch (cut off)
e. Internode
f. Wall

Figure 1.1 shows the parts of a bamboo which are standard to all species. First, what in the case of a tree is called the trunk or the stem is the *culm* of a bamboo. Usually a culm is hollow. The hollow space inside a culm is called the *cavity* (a). The cavities are separated from each other by *diaphragms* (b), which appear at the outside of the culms as *nodes* (c), where *branches* (d) leave the culm. A piece of a culm between two nodes is an *internode* (e); and, finally, we talk about the *wall* (f) of a culm.

Some of the properties determining the best use of the available bamboo are:

o   the dimensions:

- the height of the culm, which is the total height of the culm during the life of the bamboo;
- the useful length of the culm, which is the length from the bottom to a certain height where the diameter becomes too small (bamboos are tapered);
- the outer diameter at the bottom and at the top (or at the end of the useful length);

- the wall-thickness, at the same places;
- the length of the internodes (see below);

and also:

o the straightness of the culms (see below);

o the mechanical properties (see Chapter 3);

o the natural durability and the preservation (see Chapter 2);

o the useful length.

With a reasonable understanding of these data the user can select the most appropriate bamboos to use; for example, a bamboo of 20mm diameter is too thin for a beam, but appropriate for a ceiling. Similarly, the diameter of a culm can be 100mm at the bottom, and 30mm at the top. The thick lower end can be cut into pieces which are useful for housing, and the thin upper end can be used for furniture and the like.

Since most culms are not completely straight, cut them into pieces which are reasonably straight, keeping end-use requirements in mind. For building houses, lengths of 2.7m or 3m are appropriate.

When cutting a culm into pieces, it is important to pay attention to the positions of the internodes: an open end of a piece of bamboo is weak (it splits easily, and can be crushed), but a node is the strong end of a piece of bamboo.

Differences between bamboo and wood

Several differences exist between bamboo and wood. Some of them are mentioned here because they are important for the user.

o In bamboo there are no rays and no knots (a ray is the radiating part of the tissue in a tree; a knot is a hard part in timber caused by the shooting out of a branch). This makes bamboo a far more evenly stressed throughout its length.

o Bamboo is a hollow tube, sometimes with thin walls, and consequently it is more difficult to join bamboos than pieces of wood.

o Bamboo does not contain the same chemical extracts as wood, and can therefore be glued very well. However, the outer skin of a culm cannot be glued at all, because of its high silica content.

o The outer skin of a culm does not have any bark; it contains a lot of silica, which dulls the edges of tools.

Advantages and disadvantages of bamboo

Advantages:

o Because of its hollow form, bamboo is relatively strong and stiff, and it can be cut and split with simple tools.

o The surface of bamboo is hard and clean.

- o Bamboo can be grown on a village scale, or even on a family scale.

- o The return of capital is quicker than for wood.

- o Bamboo structures behave very well in storm and earthquake (see Chapter 8).

Disadvantages:

- o Low natural durability: bamboo needs preservative treatment, which in many cases is more difficult than for wood.

- o Bamboo can hardly withstand contact with the soil; however, in dry soil it can last a long time, if there are no termites.

- o Fire is a very great risk.

- o A bamboo culm is not completely straight: it is tapered; the nodes occur at different distances; the prominence of the nodes can be a nuisance when the material is being worked.

- o Standardization is virtually impossible, because of the variation in sizes. Only in the joints can an attempt at standardization be successful (see Chapter 8).

In summary, bamboo offers considerable opportunities for local people to increase their economic independence and their self-reliance. Bamboo can be grown on a small scale, preservation can be done in a small factory which does not require high investment, and building can largely be done on a self-help basis using simple tools.

Bamboo houses can be attractive, cheap and, if properly designed, long-lasting, so they represent a good choice for lower-income groups. Bamboo is also establishing itself as an industrial material. 'Plybamboo' creates many jobs and is a good export item, and parquet flooring is developing a similar importance. Furniture can be made in a small factory with light equipment.

2. Harvesting and preservation

Harvesting

Harvesting methods must take account of at least five topics: *which* culms we will harvest, *when* we will do this, *how* we will harvest them, how we will *transport* them, and how we will *store* them.

Which culms?

Only adult culms should be cut. Young culms should be left in their place, not only to grow to maturity, but mainly to provide food for the plant. It is important not to cut too many culms, otherwise damage will occur and eventually the plant will die.

A bamboo culm is ripe in three years. The age of a culm can be estimated from the colour but this depends on the botanical species. The most certain (but labour-intensive) way of knowing the age of a bamboo culm is to put a mark on all culms each year at the same place (e.g. chest-high at the roadside), preferably after new shoots have developed. If in a particular situation culms are ripe after four years then all culms with four marks can be cut.

Dead and deteriorating culms must be removed at any time, even if they are immature.

When?

Harvesting should be done in the dry season, because then the bamboo culms have a lower moisture content, making transport easier and reducing the chance of attack by fungi and rot. During the rainy (growing) season no felling should occur. According to some sources the late dry season is the best.

In some countries it is said that bamboos cut shortly after the full moon will suffer less from attack by beetles than those cut during the first two quarters. It has been discovered that the moisture content increases from full to new moon and decreases from new to full moon, but moisture content is not related to beetle attack. Only the starch content correlates with beetle attack, varying seasonally but not according to the lunar phase. The article on this subject by the researchers Kirkpatrick and Simmonds ends with the following poem:

> *Bamboo cut with moon on wane*
> *Will ensure financial gain;*
> *But beetles bore it very soon*
> *If cut upon the waxing moon;*
> *Moreover it's a well-known fact*
> *That ripe bamboo is less attacked.*

Their conclusion is that the waxing or waning of the moon does not correlate with beetle attack after cutting. However, there is no technical reason whatsoever not to follow the local belief.

How?

Usually bamboo culms are cut with a sharp machete, but for heavy culms a pruning saw or an axe can be used. In case falling causes splitting, two people should work together: one cutting the culm, the other holding it.

In densely grown plantations which are run commercially, it might be wise to use a chainsaw. The culm is cut into pieces of about 3m, while gradually being taken down.

Bamboos can be divided into two types: the clump type (pachymorph) and the running type (leptomorph). In the clump type bamboo grows in clumps of about 50 or 100 culms and in the running type the bamboo culms are evenly distributed over the area.

In the clump type the old mature culms will be found in the centre with the young ones at the circumference. An entrance has to be made to the centre which results in the horseshoe pattern (see Figure 2.1). Culms should be cut 20-30cm above ground level in order not to damage the roots, and just above a node in order to reduce splitting and avoid water collection with subsequent rot.

In the running type, bamboo culms can be cut at ground level, because the roots remain protected in the ground.

Care must be taken not to damage the skin of the culm when cutting the branches. The culms are cut into pieces of 4 to 6m long for transport, or in lengths of around 2.7 or 3m if they are to be used for housing.

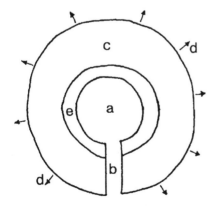

Figure 2.1: Horseshoe pattern of a bamboo clump

a. Centre of the clump
b. Entrance (and exit as well)
c. The clump in the horseshoe form
d. Direction of growth
e. Culms to be cut next time

Note: The diameter of a clump is usually 5 to 10m.

A problem with the harvest is that it is very labour intensive and requires an extensive workforce. These people are widely scattered over the forest and cannot be controlled. For casual labour, the only interest is their day's income; the next harvest is beyond their scope. This tends to result in over-cutting within short distances of the road and less or no cutting at longer distances. A reduction of productivity is the result. This will not happen if the cutters are also the owners, i.e. a co-operatively owned bamboo plantation.

Transport

Transportation methods are usually manual. The pieces of cut bamboo are carried to the roadside by head-loading, in bundles of around 10 pieces of 4m length. Once the bamboo is on the road, carts or trucks can be used. For large quantities, railway transport or river rafts might be the right solution.

Transport of bamboo is difficult:

o small quantities must be collected from a large area (e.g. 10 tonne/ha);

o difficult access;

o the walls of the fresh culms are vulnerable;

o low stacked weight per volume (e.g. 200kg/m^3).

Therefore bamboo should be used locally to avoid the need to move it long distances.

It is worthwhile to calculate the price of transport in advance as it might be cheaper to obtain bamboo from a plantation which has the easiest access.

Storage

The storage of bamboo requires special care. The ground must be clean, free of refuse of all kinds and free of termites. Bamboo should be stored under cover to protect it from rain, and clear of the ground (20 or 30cm). Good ventilation and frequent inspection are necessary. Fresh bamboo, standing vertically, will dry in four weeks; a horizontal position doubles this time. However, sometimes people are against vertical storage 'because the nature would run out of the ends'. Cracking can occur if drying takes place too quickly.

Preservation

This means:

o sound management in storage (see previous section), and in cutting time: cut the bamboo in the season when the starch content is low;

o attention to details such as keeping the bamboo dry:

   • protect the bamboo from splashing rainwater (build the roof with an over-hang),

   • allow the bamboo to dry quickly and completely after the rain has stopped,

   • avoid contact with soil (use stone foundations) etc. (see Chapter 5);

o preservation in the more narrow sense.

Before dealing with preservation we should first discuss the natural durability. This is lower than for wood and in most cases it is too low for an economic lifetime. The lifetime of untreated bamboo is:

o   in contact with atmosphere and soil: 1-3 years;

o   under cover: 4-6 years;

o   under cover and in a not very humid climate: 10-15 years.

Normally bamboo will be attacked by fungi (rot, only when moist) and insects (beetles and termites). To avoid the last, bamboo has to be treated. Unfortunately it is quite difficult to treat bamboo: the outside and inside are covered with a tight layer of cells, and the vessels through which any liquid can enter the bamboo cover only about 10 per cent of the cross-section of a culm.

The non-chemical or traditional methods will be discussed first, and then the chemical methods. All procedures should be effective, safe and economic.

Traditional methods

The advantages of these methods are that they are very cheap and can be done without special equipment.

Clump-curing The culms are cut, but left in place in a vertical position. The evaporation in the leaves reduces the starch content and consequently beetle attack. However, attack by rot and termites is not diminished.

Smoking The bamboo is stored above the fireplace. The smoke will blacken the culm and might cause cracking too. The effect on durability is doubtful.

Soaking The culms are placed (immediately after the harvest) in water or mud with stones on top of them to keep them down. They are left for several weeks and then dried over a full week (in the shade, not in the sun!).

Seasoning Bamboo has to be dry. This is achieved by drying in the open, under cover, with as much air movement as possible. It can take one or two months.

A general remark to end with: if the local population has a tradition of working with bamboo they will know best the differences in natural durability between the several local bamboos as well as the effectiveness of traditional treatments for various end uses.

Chemical treatments

Many chemicals are used as a preservative for wood or bamboo. We will deal with the most common.

CCA (copper-chrome-arsenic composition, in the proportion 3:1:4) is good for timber, but not for people. CCB and CCBF are better! (B = boron). Its commercial names include ASCU. The concentration of the solution in water (%) should be approximately the same percentage as the retention (as a guideline only), i.e. how many kilos of dry chemicals remain in $1m^3$ bamboo after treatment:

- in contact with atmosphere and soil: 8 (to 12);
- in contact with atmosphere, not soil: 5 to 8;
- under cover (trusses, purlins): 4;
- under cover (ceiling, etc.): 3.

Method: modified Boucherie process (i.e. with airpump), lasting as many hours as the percentages of retention and concentration (this again is a rough guideline).

> ### Precautions
> Most preservatives are *toxic*! Avoid contact with your skin. Wear gloves for handling the preservatives and the treated bamboos, as long as they are wet. Anyone who drinks CCA or Octabor should drink a lot of water (milk is even better) and be forced to vomit (put your fingers down his or her throat) at least three times. Consult a doctor as quickly as possible; take a package of the preservative with you and show it to the doctor.

Boric acid, borax and boron are cheaper than CCA and less poisonous. For boric acid and borax the commercial names include Octabor. The concentration of the solution is 2.5 per cent each, to be dissolved in hot water; the retention, for use under cover only, $5kg/m^3$.

For boron the full name is Octoborate disodico tetrahydrate; the concentration is 10 per cent in water.

However, both will diffuse out of bamboo when moist.

Method: open tank method, or modified Boucherie until moisture of 10 per cent of the volume of the bamboo has left the lower end.

Diesel oil is not toxic, but beetles do not like the smell. They wait until the smell has disappeared or until they are really hungry.

Three methods of treating the bamboo with these preservatives are as follows.

Open tank method

An open tank is a trough of about 4m long. This can be made by cutting two 200-litre drums in half vertically and welding them together like a canoe. Cut the drums with a cold chisel and a hammer; flatten the sharp edges with a hammer. After welding, paint the inside with bitumen, tar, or anything like that to protect the drums from corrosion.

Put the solution into the trough, using a plastic bucket. Before putting the bamboo into the trough, cut it to the required length, splitting it if required, in order not to treat bamboo which will not be used. All bamboo should be covered with preservative. Put big stones on the bamboo, enough to keep the bamboo down (Figure 2.2A).

The bamboo must soak for a full week (split bamboos three days). Cover the trough with plastic to keep the rain out, and keep children and animals away. After soaking lift the bamboo (wear gloves!) on to sticks across the trough (Figure 2.2B) and let the preservative drain back into the trough for a few hours. After that, let the bamboo dry for a week in a rack, protected from sun and rain.

A good variant for split bamboo is the dip-diffusion method: dip the bamboo for 10 minutes, as before, but in a higher concentration, and next wrap it in plastic for one week. Then season it in a vertical position for at least three days.

Treated bamboos must not be burned; the gases of such a fire are toxic. Bury them in the ground, away from wells (for example, in a pit latrine, because these are always at a safe distance from wells).

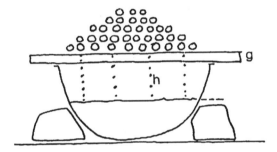

Figure 2.2: Open tank method

A. Cross-section of a trough

a. Trough with bamboos
b. Stones to keep the trough upright.
c. Level of the preservative
d. Large stones, to keep the bamboo down
e. Plastic cover against rain
f. Stones to keep e in place

B. Draining the bamboo

g. Sticks
h. Dripping preservative

Butt treatment method

The freshly cut culms should immediately be put bottom ends first into a drum containing preservative. The leaves, still in their place, act as a pump, because of the process of transpiration. After one or two weeks the preservative reaches the top; watch the change in colour of the leaves. Place the bamboos in an empty drum to regain the surplus preservative from the culms. This method can be used instead of the Boucherie when only a few culms are to be treated.

Boucherie method

This method must be applied on *fresh* bamboo, the very day the bamboos are cut (or they can be kept under water). Pressure is needed to press the preservative into the bamboo, and can be created by an airpump, or a tower. In this last case a drum containing preservative is put on a tower of 4 to 6m high and connected by tubes to the end of the bamboos (see Figure 2.3) using cuffs (see Figure 2.4). At first, sap will drip from the low end with hardly any preservative. As the process continues the concentration of preservative in this sap will steadily increase.

This sap must be collected. It can be used again if preservative is added to achieve the original concentration. The culm is ready when preservative in the original concentration drips out of the far end. This takes about one hour. Check this yourself: give the preservative a colour from which you can judge the result, or use a piece of pH (litmus) paper to check the concentration. Put the bamboos in a vertical position in an empty drum to regain any surplus of preservative from the culm. (Note: this method is not applicable to bamboos with thin walls).

Figure 2.3: Boucherie method

a. Drum on tower
b. Tube, pressure resistant
c. Valves
d. Pipe, steel or iron
e. Connecting tubes with metallic clamps
f. Bamboos
g. Drip trough

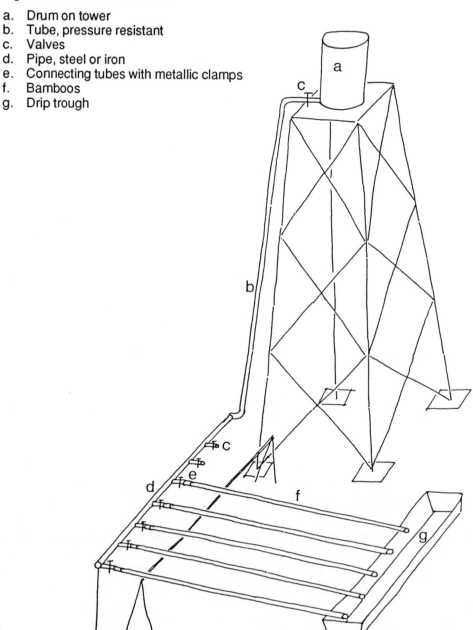

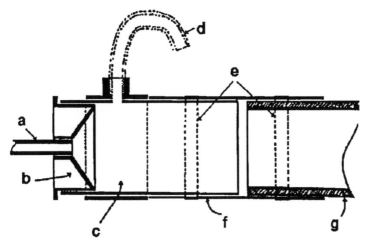

Figure 2.4: Cuff to connect bamboo

a. Entrance of liquid
b. Reduction of diameter (PVC)
c. Pressure-chamber, PVC, 100mm diameter
d. Exit of air, flexible plastic hose
e. Metal wrapping
f. Rubber sleeve
g. Bamboo culm

The economics of preservation

Generally speaking, a good (chemical) preservation can increase the natural lifetime of bamboos to 15 years in the open and 25 years under cover. Unfortunately, very few data are known about the price of preservation. The author has calculated from a real case in Africa in 1985 that preservation with Octabor in an open tank costs 30 per cent of the price of the bamboo, which is certainly economic. The same ratio has been found in Costa Rica in 1994 with boron and Boucherie: the bamboo costs $0.36 per metre, and the preservation $0.13 per metre.

For an economic use of bamboo in building it is important to pay attention to sound construction methods.

Termites

If the bamboo is likely to be attacked by termites, 1 per cent Dieldrin added to the preservative is effective. However, Dieldrin is dangerous, and use is illegal in several countries.

Note: the remaining preservative can be stored in a closed drum for another use in the near future.

3. Mechanical and economic considerations

Mechanical properties

In theory, the mechanical properties of bamboos depend on:

o   the botanical species itself;

o   the age at which the bamboo has been cut;

o   the moisture content;

o   the position along the culm (top or bottom: the bottom part of a culm is mostly used in building);

o   the position of the nodes and the internodes themselves produce different characteristics; nodes are weaker in compression and bending.

For field practitioners, however, all this can be simplified, as research carried out by the author has shown that a ratio exists between the density (mass per volume) of a piece of bamboo and the allowable stresses in it (see Table 1). A basic knowledge of mechanics is assumed.

Table 1   The ratio between the mass per volume ρ in kg/m^3 and the allowable stress in N/mm^2

	Compression (no buckling)	Bending	Shear
Dry bamboo (12% MC)	0.013	0.020	0.003
Wet or green bamboo	0.011	0.015	–

Note: Dry bamboo has a moisture content (MC) of 12 per cent when in equilibrium with air of 70 per cent relative humidity, which is a fair mean for many tropical countries. If you happen to live in a very humid climate, take the mean values of dry and wet bamboo.

Calculating the allowable stress

EXAMPLE 1

If green bamboo has a density of 600kg/m^3, then the allowable stress in bending is $0.015 \times 600 = 9$N/mm.

The problem is to determine the density of the bamboo concerned, but since this is much simpler than the determination of stresses at failure this method is really an improvement.

The density of bamboo varies between 550 and 800kg/m³. If the following method is impossible, then calculate using 550kg/m³, but this lower value is uneconomic as the allowable stress might be higher.

Determine the density as follows:

1. Cut twice at right angles through one internode of a piece of bamboo to produce a hollow bamboo cylinder with no nodes.

2. Make the following measurements accurately:

    - the height, H, in millimetres;

    - the outer diameter, D, in millimetres, twice at each end (four times in all) and calculate the mean value;

    - the wall thickness, w, in 0.1mm (using a micrometer), at each end four times (eight times in all) and calculate the mean.

3. Determine the weight, G, in grams (accurate scales might be found at a clinic, grocery store or post office).

EXAMPLE 2

(See Figure 3.1)

$$H = 292mm$$
$$D = \tfrac{1}{4} \times (82 + 81 + 83 + 82) = 82mm$$
$$w = \tfrac{1}{8} \times (6.3 + 6.4 + 6.5 + 6.4 + 6.6 + 6.4 + 6.5 + 6.5) = 6.45mm$$

The volume is:

$$H \times 3.14 (D - w) w$$
$$= 292 \times 3.14 (82 - 6.45) 6.45$$
$$= 447000mm^3$$

The weight is 272 grams.

The mass per volume (or density) is:

$$\frac{272g}{447000mm^3} = 608 \text{ kg/m}^3$$

The allowable stress for bending is (if this bamboo is dry):

$$0.020 \times 608 = 12.2 \text{ N/mm}$$

The allowable stress for any material is not a constant factor, but depends on the length of time that the force (or 'load') is applied. The shorter the duration of the load, the 'stronger' the material is. The allowable stresses given in Table 1 assume that the load is permanent; for instance the dead weight of floors, walls and roofs.

If part of the load is 'live' (e.g. inhabitants and furniture) the allowable stress and therefore the allowable load can be increased by 25 per cent while still maintaining a suitable safety margin, because part of the load is of a short duration. Similarly, if wind is likely to be the major load the allowable stresses given in Table 1 can be increased by 50 per cent, as wind-load tends to have an even shorter duration.

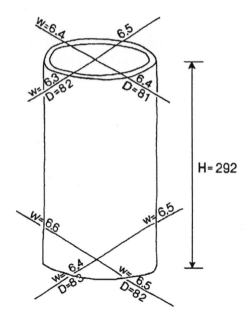

W=6.4 6.5
W=6.3 6.4
D=82   D=81

H= 292

W=6.6   W=6.5

W=6.4   W=6.5
D=83   D=82

Figure 3.1: Allowable stress

Different structures have to bear different loads and it is important to decide which is the crucial element in each case before making calculations about the strength of the structure. For a beam supporting a wall, the dead load will be the major one; for a roof, wind-load is likely to be critical; and for a bridge the main load will be live. Thus for the green bamboo in Example 1 the allowable stresses would be $9N/mm^2$ if used in a wall, $11.25N/mm^2$ if used in a bridge, and $13.5N/mm^2$ if used in a roof.

For calculations involving bending, the modulus of the cross-section of the bamboo, W, must be calculated. (The modulus of the cross-section is defined as the area moment of inertia divided by the greatest depth of the section; in the case of a hollow circular section, its radius.) This is because the maximum bending stress, σ (sigma) N/mm^2, equals the bending moment, M Nmm, divided by the modulus of the cross-section, Wmm^3. W can be calculated as a function of D and w (see Table 2).

Table 2 The modulus of section W (mm^3) as a function of outer diameter D and wall thickness w

w(mm)	4	5	6	7	8	9	10
D(mm)							
50	6000	7200	8000				
60		11000	12700	14000			
70		15400	17700	20000	21700		
80			24000	27000	29700	32200	
90				35100	38900	42200	45300
100				44400	49200	53800	58000

Note: Bamboos are tapered; if the length is 3m or less, take the mean value of both ends, but if the bamboos are longer, take the mean value minus 15 per cent.

14

EXAMPLE 3

A footbridge is to be built with a free span of 4m, using bamboos with a mean outside diameter of 90mm. The wall thickness in the middle of the length of the bamboo cannot be measured; at one end it is 7.8mm and at the other 6.2mm, so assume the thickness in the middle is the mean of the two, i.e. 7.0mm.

To calculate the uniformly distributed load (q N/mm) which one bamboo, length L mm, supported only at its ends, can carry, the formula $q = 8M/L^2$ is used, where $M = \sigma \times W$, in Nmm.

As the bridge is merely a footbridge, it can be assumed that the dead weight is negligible. Assuming that the bamboo is the same as that measured in Example 2, the allowable stress is therefore $1.25 \times 12.2 = 15.2 \text{N/mm}^2$.

From Table 2:
$$M = \sigma W = 15.2 \times 35100$$
$$= 535000 \text{ Nmm}$$

Allowable load
$$= q = 8M/L^2 \text{ (M in Nmm, L in mm)}$$
$$= \frac{8 \times 535000}{(4000)^2}$$
$$= 0.267 \text{ N/mm}$$

Assuming a uniformly distributed live load on the bridge of 1 N/mm (i.e. people, 750N each, walking with a distance of 0.75m between them), 4 bamboos will be needed (4 is 1 divided by 0.267 and corrected to the nearest whole number above it). The bamboos should be tightly joined together and the supports should be made at a node or as close to one as possible.

In most cases this calculation of the strength is sufficient, but sometimes it may be necessary to calculate the deformation as well. The necessary formulae are:

For a uniformly distributed load, q N/mm:

$$f = \frac{5}{384} \times \frac{qL^4}{EI} \text{ mm}$$

For a concentrated load, F N:

$$f = \frac{FL^3}{48EI}$$

in which
$$
\begin{aligned}
f &= \text{deformation in mid-span (mm)} \\
q &= \text{uniformly distributed load (N/mm)} \\
F &= \text{load concentrated at one point (N)} \\
L &= \text{span (mm)} \\
E &= \text{Young's Modulus (N/mm}^2) \\
I &= \text{area moment of inertia (mm}^4)
\end{aligned}
$$

For bamboo $E = 20000$ N/mm^2 and the formulae can be simplified to:

(for a uniformly distributed load)

$\quad$ f $\quad$ = $\quad$ $10L^2\,\sigma/D$ mm

(for a concentrated load)

$\quad$ f $\quad$ = $\quad$ $8.L^2\,\sigma/D$ mm

in which

$\quad$ L $\quad$ = $\quad$ free span (metres)
$\quad$ D $\quad$ = $\quad$ outer diameter (mm)
$\quad$ σ $\quad$ = $\quad$ actual stress (N/mm^2).

In this example the actual stress is:

$$\sigma \; = \; \frac{M}{W} \; = \; qL^2/8W = \; \frac{1 \times 4000^2}{8 \times 4 \times 35100} \; = \; 14.25 \text{ N/mm}^2$$

(*Note*: the 4 is the number of bamboos)

$\quad$ and the deformation is:

$$f \quad = \quad \frac{10 \times 4^2 \times 14.25}{90} \; = 25\text{mm}$$

In practice a good guideline is to limit the deformation to 1/300 of the span. To achieve this, the stress should be limited to:

(for a distributed load)

$$\sigma \; = \; \frac{\text{Outer diameter in mm}}{3 \times \text{span in metres}}$$

(for a concentrated load)

$$\sigma \; = \; \frac{\text{Outer diameter in mm}}{2.5 \times \text{span in metres}}$$

For the bridge in the example:

$$\sigma \; = \; \frac{90}{3 \times 4} \; = 7.50 \text{ N/mm}^2$$

This is the stress allowable in each bamboo to give the required stiffness, from which follows:

$$M \; = \; \sigma W = 7.50 \times 35100 = 263000 \text{ Nmm}$$

$$q \; = \; 8M/L^2 = \frac{8 \times 263000}{4000^2} = 0.132 \text{ N/mm}$$

To bear 1N/mm, 7 bamboos (each with a load-bearing capacity of 0.132N/mm) should be sufficient if tightly lashed together.

Economics

An important consideration for most people is whether bamboo is cheaper than timber or not. For a simple case, like a beam or a column, one can compare prices as follows.

Suppose that in your country the price of bamboo is A coins per culm and the price of timber is B coins per m^3 (A and B are prices in the local currency). Firstly, calculate the content in m^3 for the bamboo culm:

$$\frac{\pi}{4} (D^2 - d^2) \text{ L in which:}$$

π = 3.14
D = outer diameter (mean)
d = inner diameter (mean)
L = length

For example: $\pi/4 \times (0.100^2 - 0.088^2) \times 8 = 0.014 \ m^3$ for a culm with outer diameter 100mm, wall thickness 6mm and length 8m. The price per m^3 appears to be:

$1/0.014 = 70$ A.

However, the hollow form of bamboo means that it is twice as effective as timber. (Technicians would say the ratio of the moment of inertia to the cross-section for a hollow tube is twice that for a massive, rectangular or square cross-section.)

Consequently, we can assume a price of $35A/m^3$ for bamboo, to be compared with B/m^3 for timber.

Some presuppositions:

o The lifetime is the same; therefore you have to preserve the bamboo, and you have to calculate the price of preserved bamboo.

o The details of a bamboo building differ very much from those of a timber building, and this influences the price considerably. In fact, two estimates are necessary, one for the building in bamboo, and another for the building in timber. The above method might be very helpful for a first impression.

4. Housing in general

Although a house can be built completely of bamboo (except for the fireplace and the chimney), usually bamboo is combined with other building materials such as timber, clay, or roofing sheets, according to their availability, suitability, and cost.

Most bamboo houses are characterized by a mediocre level of design and execution, but in Japan, for example, bamboo is being used for expensive and beautiful houses for the upper class. With a similar level of design, attractive houses can be built for lower-income groups. In Costa Rica some hundreds of houses have been built recently for low-income groups.

The architect must be aware of the possibilities of bamboo regarding strength, beauty and processing. The design of a bamboo house has to meet cultural and social patterns, the demands of the climate, and so on.

First considerations

The frame of the house consists of the floorbeams, the columns and the trusses and purlins. A bamboo frame keeps its shape very well in case of an earthquake (see Chapter 8). However, most earthquakes are followed by fire caused by stoves and paraffin lamps falling over. Such a fire might cause more damage than the earthquake. It is wise to take precautions: make stoves and lamps stable, and use incombustible materials around the fireplace.

For the frame, only whole (i.e. full cross-section) bamboo culms are generally used. However, new ideas tend to advocate the use of split bamboos (e.g. 6mm thick and 40mm wide) to compose the frame. This opens the way to standardization. Normally, bamboos are tapered, and the top parts are thin-walled as well. It is common practice to use the lower parts of the culms for the frame, and keep the upper parts for walls, ceilings, furniture and the like.

The basic problem is how to join the columns with the floorbeams and the trusses. Joints like those for timber are not appropriate; a mortise-and-tenon joint, for example, cuts away the wall of the culm, and connects only the cavities inside. In Chapters 5 (floors) and 8 (trusses) bamboo joints will be described in detail.

Nails will cause the splitting of most bamboos; only a few species can be nailed. Bamboo joints are usually held together with lashes (of sisal, rattan, coconut fibre, etc.). Bolts or wooden pins can also be used. However, normally the strength and stiffness of the bamboo will be spoiled by such joints.

Note: If strong winds or earthquakes occur in the region, the frame of the house should be stiffened in two horizontal directions with diagonals between the columns and the beams.

Safety

Anyone who builds a house meets a series of hazards:

- o   wind (see Chapter 8);
- o   earthquake, in which case a bamboo house behaves well;
- o   rats and termites (see Chapters 5 and 7);
- o   rot and fungi (see Chapter 2);
- o   and fire, which will be dealt with here.

Fire is a considerable risk in bamboo. The best text on this subject is the lecture given by the late C.H. Duff in Shanghai, 1940:

> Bamboo and matting structures have a very bad fire record. Although the solid material of the wall of the bamboo, when subjected to heat, does not appear to ignite any more readily than timber, the combination of bamboo and matting has proved to be hazardous. A fire, once started, spreads rapidly up the sides of the shed and soon destroys the joint lashings, causing an early collapse of the structure. Subsequent bursting of the closed cavities between the nodes of the bamboo poles, due to steam pressure, speeds up the rate of combustion and causes burning embers to travel some considerable distance.
>
> One of the worst fire tragedies occurred many years ago in Canton when a typical South China matshed theatre seating over 2000 people caught fire during a performance, resulting in the death of 1600 persons. In 1917, a long narrow three-storey bamboo and matting structure, which was built as a temporary additional grandstand on the Hongkong Race Course to accommodate 2000 people, caught fire and collapsed with a consequent death toll of about 500 persons. It should be pointed out, however, that in both of these cases, the means of egress were hopelessly inadequate. The ordinary single-storey matshed can be quickly vacated at almost any point through the flimsy matting wall.

Later on in his lecture Mr Duff pointed out that plastering on both sides of a bamboo wall is the best way of avoiding fire. However, fire will be no problem in bamboo housing if only the following precautions are taken.

- o   Cooking should be done outside; if it is done inside, then there should be a safe cooking place with a safe chimney (i.e. surrounded by any non-combustible material).

- o   Cover the roof with a non-combustible material, such as galvanized iron roofing sheets, fibre-cement roofing sheets or tiles, or plaster. Keep in mind that an organic material (such as bamboo or grass) is likely to spread a fire.

- o   A single-storey building can be vacated simply; for buildings with two storeys or more, a good and easy escape has to be provided.

- o   Keep some distance between bamboo buildings, and keep this space clear and free from combustible waste.

Fire-resisting treatments, consisting of impregnation with chemicals, are rather expensive; moreover, they are said not to be effective.

5. Floors and foundations

Some bamboo houses have no floor other than the surface of the earth on which they have been built. This surface should be raised with earth to keep it dry. Such a floor might be covered with bamboo mats (see below). The soil has to be graded first, and compacted. Another working method is to grade the soil, to lay the bamboo mats and only then to pound them with a tamper, in order to get a close contact between the mats and the soil.

In better houses, the floor is raised above the ground level. Such a floor is more hygienic. It consists of supporting beams (part of the frame of the house), joists and a floor covering, all made of bamboo. The distance between the joists and the ground level should be at least 500mm to allow inspection of the floor joists. Other possible uses for the space below the floor include storage, the keeping of domestic animals, or a children's playground. On sloping ground it is of course necessary to raise the floor.

Be careful: do not give rats the opportunity to make nests unseen! See Figure 5.1.

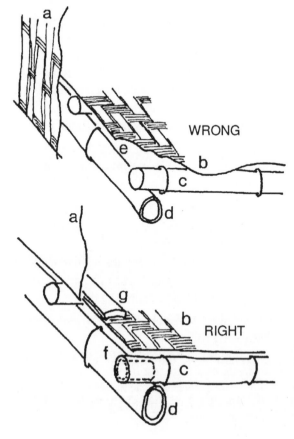

Figure 5.1: How to avoid rats' nests in a floor

a. Wall (woven bamboo)
b. Floorcover (woven bamboo)
c. Joist
d. Beam
e. Space for rats' nests. Wrong!
f. Correct solution: Bamboo wall ends above the joist; joists are shut off with wooden plugs
g. Split bamboo, to fasten floor and wall

20

Foundations

Bamboo in contact with the soil has a very short lifetime. A foundation should therefore be made with concrete, stone or brick. The foundation must of course be strong enough to keep the house upright, but it has also to keep the house down in case of strong wind. Do not forget to anchor the house to the foundation! (See Figure 5.2.)

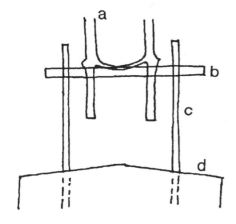

Figure 5.2: Foundation, vertical cross-section

a. Bamboo column, e.g. ϕ 100mm and thick-walled
b. Steel pin, e.g. ϕ 12mm
c. Steel strip, e.g. 3 × 40mm, U-shaped, as deep into the concrete as possible
d. Concrete foundation, e.g. 300 × 300mm, actual size depends on local soil conditions

If termites occur, keep a free space between the bamboo and the concrete, and whitewash the concrete. If termites are a persistent problem, books are available which cover the subject in detail (see Further reading section).

The column (a) in Figure 5.2 might have a short lifetime due to splashing rainwater. Make the lower end of the column exchangeable (see Figure 5.3).

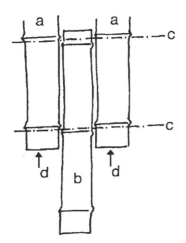

Figure 5.3: Exchangeable lower end of column

a. Column of the house, double, e.g. 2 × ϕ 100mm
b. Exchangeable bamboo part, which is the same as part a in Figure 5.2; a piece of hardwood might be a good solution
c. Two steel pins ϕ 12mm or hardwood pins ϕ 25mm (note the positions of the nodes)
d. If b has to be renewed, support the house temporarily here

The National Bamboo Project in Costa Rica has developed a very clever and simple foundation for a bamboo column, as shown in Figure 5.4.

Cut a bamboo in such a way that the lower end is open for 0.3m up to the first node, or remove one of the lower nodes. Take a plastic tube (like one for waste water) which is wider than the bamboo, about 1.3m long. Cut it open with a sharp knife from one end to the other, and wrap it round the 0.3m at the lower end of the bamboo, and fasten

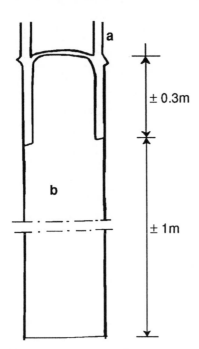

Figure 5.4: Foundation, vertical cross-section

a. Bamboo, e.g. part *b* in Figure 5.3
b. Concrete, poured in *a,* upside down

it tight with iron wire. The plastic will fold itself around the bamboo. Also wrap iron wire around the remaining metre of plastic tube which extends beyond the bamboo, until it is all the same diameter. Turn it upside down and pour concrete in it. The next day you can remove the plastic tube and reuse it. The result is a bamboo culm elongated by one metre of concrete of the same diameter, which makes a simple and effective foundation. Prefabrication is possible.

Joints of beam and column

Generally, one has to be careful with bamboo fittings, if these are based on some sort of penetration, like pins. Bamboo is weakened by the stresses caused by such fittings. It is important to study examples like those in Figures 5.2 and 5.3, keeping in mind that the weight of the house is acting downwards, and derive from Figure 5.3 the position of the nodes. For upward (wind) forces it should be the other way. Avoid penetration of bamboos as much as possible.

If the column ends, the beam can simply be supported (see Figure 5.5A). Usually, the column has to pass along the beam. Basically, two solutions are possible, as shown in Figures 5.5B and 5.5C.

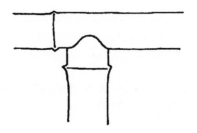 

Figure 5.5A: Beam on top of column

22

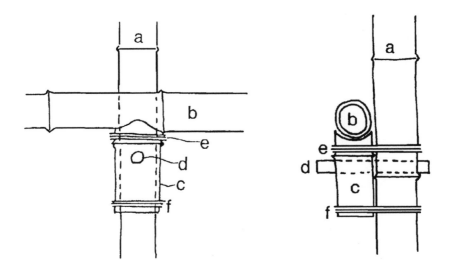

Figure 5.5B: Joint of column and beam

a. Column, e.g. φ 100mm
b. Beam (kept in place with lashing, omitted in order to keep the drawing clear)
c. Supporting piece, thick-walled
d. Pin of hardwood, e.g. φ 30mm (note the position of the nodes)
e. Lashing, to keep *c* in place
f. Lashing; this one can be a pin as well

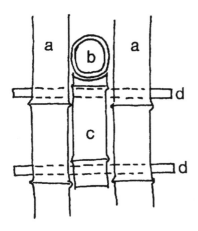

Figure 5.5C: Beam between double column

Joints of joist and beam

Usually, joists are laid on the beams without any mechanical connection. However, it is better to join them with lashings (Figure 5.6A). Sometimes hardwood pins are used (Figure 5.6B), or a split bamboo is put through the joists, and is lashed to the beam (Figure 5.6C).

The distance of the joists has to be calculated (see Chapter 3). As far as the floor covering is concerned, the maximum distance is normally 400mm.

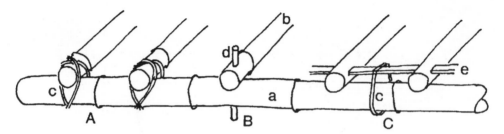

Figure 5.6: Joists on beam

A. With lashings
B. With pins
C. With split bamboo
a. Beam

b. Joists
c. Lashings
d. Wooden pin
e. Split bamboo

Floor covering

A floor cover, made out of flattened bamboo, woven bamboo, split bamboo, or small bamboos, is laid on top of the joists.

Flattened bamboo

A green bamboo culm is cut open on one side with a knife, and then it is unfolded until flat. The diaphragms are removed. A bamboo of diameter 100mm produces a flattened bamboo of about 320mm wide. This is laid on top of the joists, and lashed to them or nailed (see Figure 5.7A).

Woven bamboo

This will be dealt with in detail in Chapter 11. A floor detail is shown in Figure 5.7B. A floor like this is fastened only as in Figure 5.1, item g.

Split bamboo

Sometimes a timber lath is nailed on top of the bamboo joists, to enable the floor to be nailed in its turn (see Figure 5.7C).

Small bamboos (or cane)

These are shown in Figure 5.7D. Depending on their diameter, the distance of the joists can be greater; up to 500 or 600mm. A timber lath might be added.

Floors like A and D are sometimes covered with a layer of cement mortar to meet hygiene requirements or to provide comfort if the night is cool. In case of an earthquake this cement will cause a horizontal force on the substructure.

Modern developments

Traditionally, bamboo joints are made most of the time with pins and open ends, kept together with a rope, with the result that the strength of the bamboo is lost in the joint, and deformation is considerable. Modern research by Dr Oscar Arce from Costa Rica

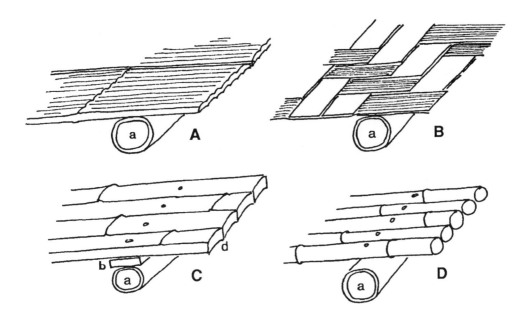

Figure 5.7: Floor covering

A. Flattened bamboos
B. Woven bamboo
C. Split bamboos
D. Small bamboos, joists at greater distance

a. Joists, 400mm centre-on-centre maximum
b. Timber lath, to facilitate nailing

has shown a different way. His option is to look for a type of joint in which the strength of the bamboo is kept, and deformation is little.

He first considers the properties of the material:

o strong in the direction of the axis;

o weak in a perpendicular direction;

o can be split easily;

o open ends are easily crushed;

o not exactly round;

o not exactly straight.

Next, he formulates the requirements for the construction:

o simple;

o stable;

o modular system, which allows for prefabrication and mass production;

o strength is predictable;

o cost effective.

His design philosophy is to make full use of the advantages of bamboo, and to avoid the negative aspects. This results in the following recommendations.

o   Avoid penetration by nails, screws and bolts.

o   Avoid open ends.

o   Take into account that bamboo is not perfectly round or straight.

o   Make use of the axial strength.

Finally, his proposal is to glue a cylindrical piece of wood internally to the culm (see Figure 5.8). Advantages are:

o   No harm is done to the bamboo.

o   The open end is filled.

o   Bamboos which are not round and not straight are not a problem.

o   Near the joint, the bamboo is strengthened by the wood.

o   The wooden pieces can be mass-fabricated.

o   All methods of joining wood are now available.

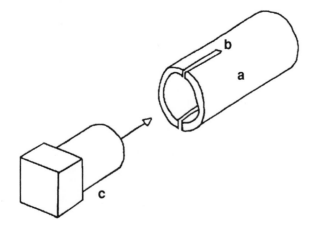

Figure 5.8: Device for joining bamboos

a.   Bamboo culm
b.   Slot
c.   Wood, glued inside the bamboo

Two slots are sawn into the bamboo, as shown in the figure, to control cracking, as bamboo is rarely perfectly round. The inner surface must be carefully cleaned before glueing, using a hand-held drill with a piece of sandpaper attached to the bit. Up to 5mm can easily be removed this way.

The idea is to make the wooden pieces in a workshop, with a lath. This simplifies the construction process in the field considerably. Wood pieces of the required diameter can be obtained from plantation thinnings.

6. Walls, doors and windows

Walls

The function of a wall is to protect from rain, wind, sun, theft, etc. and eventually to support the roof. The wall has to contain bracing to resist hurricanes and earthquakes, and this framework can be filled in as follows:

- o *Woven bamboo*, in many variations (see Chapter 11). Avoid a cavity in order to control rats; if you like to use a double bamboo mat, fasten them with laths at 250mm intervals.

- o *Vertical bamboos*, either whole culms like the floor covering in Figure 5.7D or longitudinal halves (see Figure 6.1). The bamboos dry more quickly after rain in a vertical position than in a horizontal position.

- o *Flattened bamboos*, like the floor covering in Figure 5.7A (page 25). These flattened bamboos are fastened to the columns as in Figure 6.2.

- o The vertical and flattened bamboos can be plastered with mud or cement plaster; this is the so-called 'wattle-and-daub wall' (in South America this is called *Quincha*): see Figure 6.3, which shows an example with woven bamboo.

- o Finally, in Figure 6.4, the South-American *Bajareque wall* is shown: bamboo strips are nailed or lashed on both sides of the columns. The cavity is filled with mud and stones, and both sides of the wall are plastered with mud or cement mortar. However, the amount of bamboo in such a wall is enough to burn the mud into bricks, with a much longer lifetime!

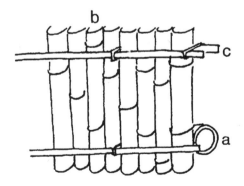

Figure 6.1: Wall of vertical bamboos

a. Beam
b. Bamboo halves
c. Split bamboos, and lashings

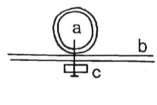
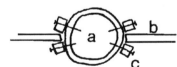

Figure 6.2: Horizontal cross-sections

a. Column
b. Flattened bamboos
c. Laths (usually hardwood) and nails

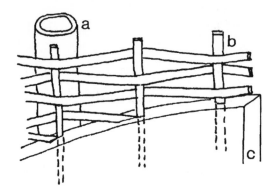

Figure 6.3: Wattle-and-daub wall
a. Column
b. Bamboo, woven with intervals
c. Plaster

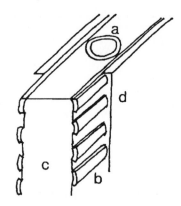

Figure 6.4: Bajareque wall
a. Column
b. Split bamboos
c. Mud
d. Plaster

Doors and windows

Usually doors and windows in bamboo houses are very simple. Doors are side-hinged, and they may consist of a bamboo frame with a panel of woven bamboo (Figure 6.5). Windows are left unglazed. Only when the walls are plastered are wooden doors and glazed windows seen, in order to meet climatic needs and to protect from theft. Glazed windows must be made from wood.

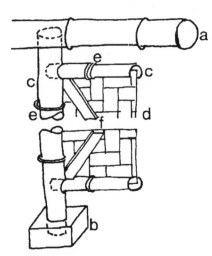

Figure 6.5: Components of a bamboo door
a. Lintel
b. Wooden block as lower hinge
c. Bamboo frame with a slot for the infill
d. Woven bamboo
e. Lashings to keep *c* tight
f. Bracing

An unglazed bamboo window might be filled in with bamboo bars (Figure 6.6) or it might be a frame with woven bamboo (Figure 6.7), hinged at the top. In daytime this serves to exclude sunshine and rainfall; at night it can be closed to keep out mosquitos etc. Sliding windows are a solution too: see Figure 6.8.

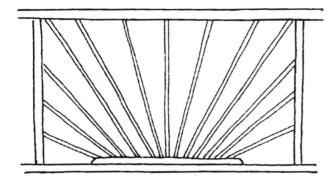

Figure 6.6: Bamboo window

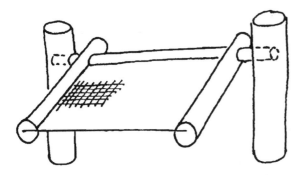

Figure 6.7: Bamboo window hinged at the top

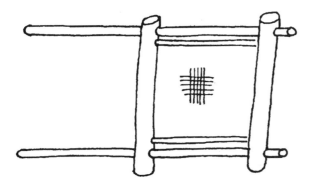

Figure 6.8: Sliding window

7. Roofs and ceilings

Roofs

A bamboo roof can be seen as a system of purlins, rafters and tile-laths, bearing a roof-cover made of tiles, sheets, grass or palm leaves. The bamboo structure is nailed or lashed. A bamboo roof may also be constructed as the covering of the building. In this case the lifetime becomes a problem, because the bamboo cover is exposed to all weather conditions and even if preserved it will last on average only two years.

There are three main types of bamboo roof cover.

o   *Halved bamboos*, all running from the ridge to the lower end of the roof

In the first layer bamboos are laid right next to each other with the curved sides down; next the top layer is laid with the curved side up (see Figure 7.1).

All bamboos are lashed or nailed to the purlins. Their diameter is 80mm or more. The weight of such a roof-cover is 20kg per m^2. A gutter is unusual; a bamboo roof is built with an overhang of say one metre, and the rainwater can drip freely from the bottom edge of the roof. Sometimes a gutter is used to keep all the bamboos together, but in the case of heavy rainfall this gutter will overflow.

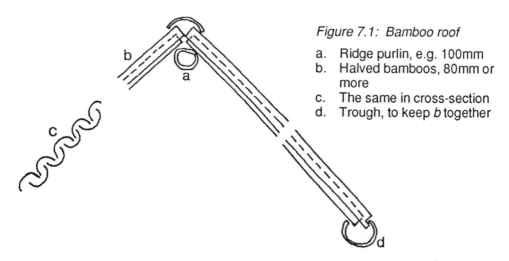

Figure 7.1: Bamboo roof

a.   Ridge purlin, e.g. 100mm
b.   Halved bamboos, 80mm or more
c.   The same in cross-section
d.   Trough, to keep *b* together

o   *Bamboo shingles*, cut from mature but still green culms, of a diameter as great as possible (e.g. 150mm).

The shingles are 40mm wide and as long as the distance between the nodes (e.g. 400 to 600mm). A hanging split is cut into each shingle, with which the shingle is hooked to the lath. Additional nailing is necessary if high wind speeds occur. For a watertight roof three layers of shingles are necessary, resulting in a roof with a weight of about 20 or 25kg per m². After their lifetime as shingles has finished, they might serve well as firewood for cooking.

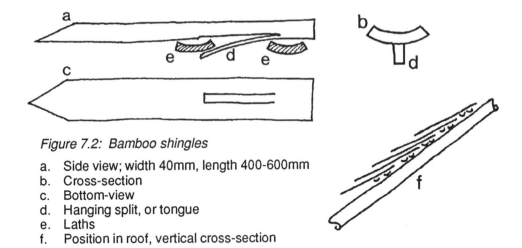

Figure 7.2: Bamboo shingles

a. Side view; width 40mm, length 400-600mm
b. Cross-section
c. Bottom-view
d. Hanging split, or tongue
e. Laths
f. Position in roof, vertical cross-section

o   In Colombia, bamboo roofs are made from *bamboos covered with a layer of cement mortar* (1 cement: 2 sand), with chopped fibres added.

Note 1 In all cases, the details of any roof should be designed in such a way that the inhabitants can check any part of the roof easily. If some hidden places occur (e.g. where a truss, a ridge purlin and two rafters meet), rats' nests are likely to be built.
Note 2 A bamboo roof is a great risk as far as fire is concerned: see Chapter 4.

Ceilings

It depends on local cultural practice whether or not a ceiling will be built. A ceiling can protect the inhabitants from heat radiation during a sunny day (Figure 7.3), and an airstream between roof and ceiling can cool the house considerably. Sometimes the ceiling is omitted, facilitating the disposal of smoke from an open indoor kitchen fire, and providing more free height inside the house.

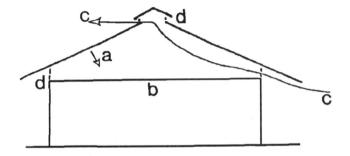

Figure 7.3: Cross-section of a building with a ceiling

a. Heat radiation from the roof
b. Ceiling
c. Airstream
d. Air inlet with mosquito mesh

A bamboo ceiling can be made from small bamboos, closely placed, from woven bamboo, or from flattened bamboo. Details are similar as those for floors (see Figure 5.7). Sometimes such a ceiling is placed on top of the purlins, covered with galvanized iron sheets (see Figure 7.4).

Be careful to check the space on top of the ceiling for rats' nests regularly.

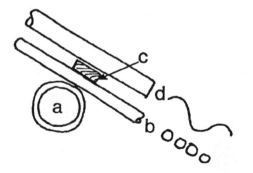

Figure 7.4: Ceiling on top of purlins

a. Purlin
b. Ceiling
c. Wooden lath
d. Roofing sheet

8. Trusses

Bamboo trusses are constructions which can be used to support the roofs of buildings such as houses, schools, medical centres and crop stores; this chapter discusses those with a 'free' (i.e. unsupported) span of eight or more metres.

In many regions where bamboo is a familiar building material, such trusses are in traditional use but they are often built with more bamboo than is necessary and are at the same time not always structurally sound.

The correct construction of trusses made with steel or timber can be calculated using data from handbooks or building regulations. In the case of bamboo, however, designers have to design and test their own trusses.

For example, a research programme has been carried out at the Eindhoven University of Technology, studying the use of trusses with a free span of eight metres to support a roof of galvanized metal or fibre-cement corrugated sheets.

The well-known king-post type of truss (Figure 8.1) was tested in this programme and an improved layout (Figure 8.2) has been developed. (As the truss is shown in cross-section, the purlins, which run horizontally under the length of the roof supporting it, appear as small circles.) The strength of this new layout is better, and the deformation is less, though more bamboo is needed and more joints have to be made. The photograph shows the truss being tested. The truss is laid down on the floor of the lab.

In this chapter some designs for making joints will be discussed, and criteria for selecting a joint, as well as the mechanical behaviour of a truss as a whole.

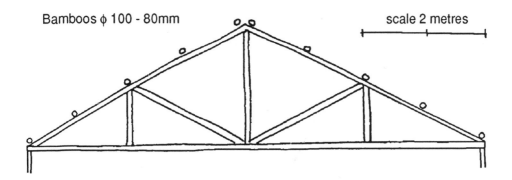

Bamboos φ 100 - 80mm   scale 2 metres

Figure 8.1: King-post type truss

33

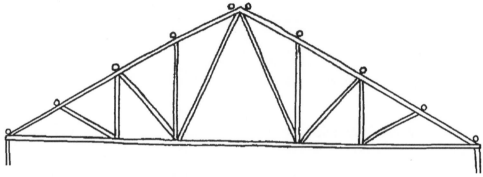

Figure 8.2: Improved type truss

The truss being
tested

Anybody who wishes to design and build bamboo trusses should be familiar with mechanics and structural design. This means, for example, keeping in mind the different types of loads:

o the permanent load of the truss's own weight;

o temporary loads such as wind;

o and loads during construction.

Each has its own allowable stress, which is low for permanent loads and higher for short-term loads.

Similarly, deformation has to be predicted. Normally this can be determined with a loading test, but in the long term deformation will be two or three times as much as the deformation in a short-term loading test.

Joints

Joint 1 (see Figure 8.3)

This joint is built with plywood (*a*) on both sides of the bamboo, and steel bolts (*b*) throughout. It is a very strong and stiff joint, but the use of plywood and steel bolts might be expensive.

The purlin rests on the plywood, but to resist wind suction it must be fastened with bolts or lashes, otherwise the roof will be lifted from the truss as soon as the wind speed exceeds about 20m/s (a moderate wind).

It is important to place the joint in a bamboo structure in such a way that a joint is made either at a node or as near to a node as possible.

An advantage of this joint, and of joint 4, is that a series can be prefabricated; in most other joints the bamboos have to fit precisely, but in this case the plywood does the job. As bamboo is not straight, precise fitting can be difficult.

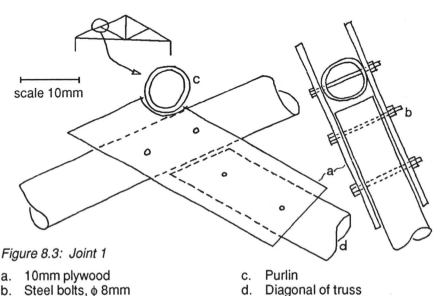

scale 10mm

Figure 8.3: Joint 1

a. 10mm plywood   c. Purlin
b. Steel bolts, φ 8mm   d. Diagonal of truss

Joint 2 (see Figure 8.4)

In this joint the diagonal (a) rests against three pins (b), which are inserted through the upper member (c). The pins have two functions: they support both the purlin (d) and the diagonal. A split bamboo as an intermediate layer (e) on both sides of the upper member prevents it from being penetrated by the purlin or the diagonal. This simple detail improves the strength considerably.

The form of these pins provides a better support for the purlin, and prevents the pins from falling down on to the floor. To be kept in place, the intermediate layers fit around the pins.

The lashings (f) can be made with, for example, 5mm sisal rope; they are drawn as a single line, but each line symbolizes three ropes. The reason for this rope is wind suction: the compression force in the diagonal changes into a tensile force.

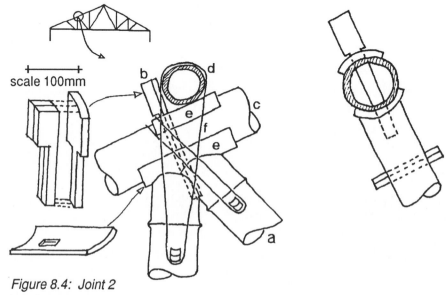

Figure 8.4: Joint 2

a. Diagonal
b. Pins
c. Upper member

d. Purlin
e. Intermediate layer
f. Lashings

Joint 3 (see Figure 8.5)

Joint 3 is based on two 'horns' (a) at the end of the diagonal (b), which enter two holes (d) in the upper member (c). The joint is lashed with rope. Horns like these are a very traditional method of joining bamboos, but they do not appear to have been tested for strength until recently. The strength is rather low.

A disadvantage of this joint is that the diagonal has to fit exactly at both ends on to the upper and lower members of the truss. This requires craftmanship and time, and impedes prefabrication. The upper and lower members should have nodes as close as possible to the joint.

The vertical fits simply in between, and is lashed. Horns are not necessary because the forces in a vertical are smaller than in a diagonal. The vertical is not shown in the detail, in order to keep the diagram clear.

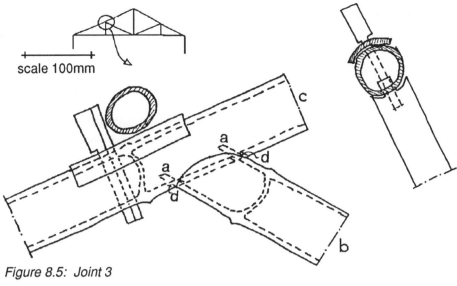

scale 100mm

Figure 8.5: Joint 3

a. Horns
b. Diagonal

c. Upper member
d. Holes

Joint 4 (see Figure 8.6)

This is based on the principle of a truss with double upper and lower members (a) and single verticals and diagonals (b) fitting in between them. The bamboos are held together by bamboo 'pins' (c) which pass through all three. Prefabrication is possible. At each joint a hole is drilled through all three bamboos and this hole is made square with a rasp to allow the bamboo pins to fit in. This joint can be made with a steel bolt instead of a bamboo pin, and the steel bolt version has been used for a century in bridge construction.

The purlin should be lashed, and the double members should be kept together with lashes as well.

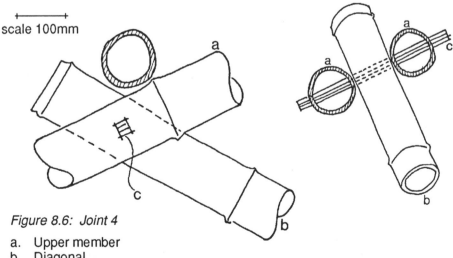

scale 100mm

Figure 8.6: Joint 4

a. Upper member
b. Diagonal
c. Pins, 7 × 10mm each

37

Joint 5 (see Figure 8.7)

Figure 8.7 shows a truss, designed and tested in Bangladesh in 1986 by Mr Eriksen from Danida. It is based on steel dowels and galvanized wire. It is able to carry a roof with burnt clay tiles, a heavy load. The allowable load is 360 N/m' (Newtons per metre length) with a 6m free span.

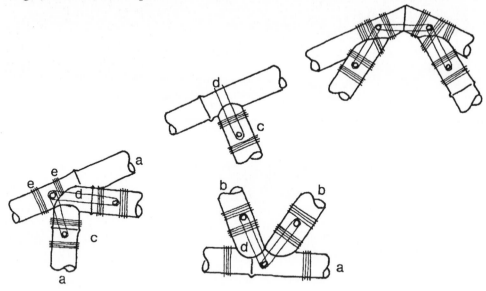

Figure 8.7: Bamboo truss, span 6m, for tiles

a. Bamboos φ 100mm
b. Bamboos φ 80mm
c. Steel dowels φ 8mm, 150mm long
d. Galvanized wire, φ 1.5mm, 10 times around, twisted, and fixed with a nail

(because during loading it tends to return to its original shape)
e. Galvanized wire, φ 2mm, 4 times around on both sides of each dowel to avoid splitting

Joint 6 (see photograph)

The photograph shows a clever design for a joint. In 1987 the author came across this design at the Instituto Tecnologico in Cartago, Costa Rica (ITCR). A piece of plywood is glued into slots which have been sawn into the ends of the bamboos. The strength and stiffness look promising. During hardening of the glue, the bamboos are wrapped stiffly with a steel band, similar to those used to connect a rubber tube to a valve. A disadvantage is the open end of the bamboos, allowing insects inside. Prefabrication is possible.

Joint 7 (see Figure 8.8)

This joint has been developed by Dr Oscar Arce from ITCR, and is shown in Chapter 5, Figure 5.8. It is stronger than joint 6: the open ends are massively filled with wood. No insect can enter the bamboo and the wood allows for any type of wood joint, as shown in Figure 8.10: steel plates, nailed or screwed on both sides.

Joint 6, designed by ITCR (the scale on top is 170mm long)

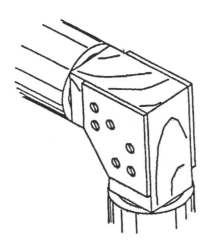

Figure 8.8: Bamboo joint with wooden infill and steel plates

Joint 8 (see Figure 8.9)

This joint has been developed by Mr Das from the Bhagalpur College of Engineering in India, in 1990. The principle is to fit a steel clamp around the bamboo, with two steel 'ears' on one side (see Figure 8.9). Bamboos can be jointed to one another by a bolt through two or more of these ears. Clamps can also be connected with a steel strip.

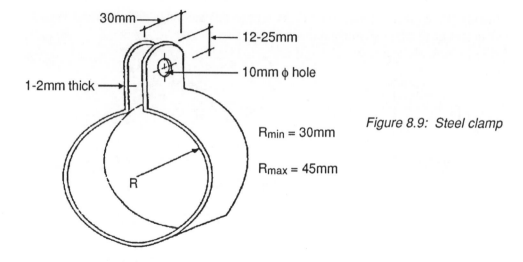

30mm

12-25mm

10mm φ hole

1-2mm thick

R_{min} = 30mm

R_{max} = 45mm

R

Figure 8.9: Steel clamp

Joint 9 (see Figure 8.10)

This joint, developed by Dr Jorge Gutierrez of Proyecto Nacional de Bambú, Costa Rica, is based on the philosophy that bamboo is good in compression and bending but weak in transition of tension forces from one bamboo to the next. Consequently, he uses the bamboo itself for compression and bending, but he pushes a steel bar through the centre of the bamboo. On both ends a steel plate is welded on to this steel bar, and the protruding ends of the bar can be welded together in order to make a joint. Domes have been built using this joint.

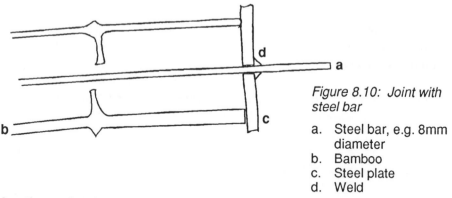

d

a

b

c

Figure 8.10: Joint with steel bar

a. Steel bar, e.g. 8mm diameter
b. Bamboo
c. Steel plate
d. Weld

Selection criteria

These joints are given as examples of what has been invented. It is a selection only; many more joints can be designed, and many more can be found in handbooks.

The problem is how to select the best joint to meet particular needs. One has to start with an inventory of these needs, and of those things which are possible locally or completely impossible.

On page 25 there is a list of items to consider while doing this exercise. Please be aware that each of the given joints has gone a long way, with many dissatisfactions and difficulties.

Finally, Figure 8.11 shows some cross-sections of buildings with bamboo trusses, just to stimulate the reader in making new designs.

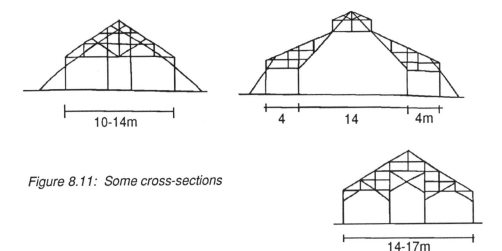

Figure 8.11: Some cross-sections

Special considerations

Mechanical behaviour of trusses

Trusses have to be tested at full scale before they can be applied in buildings. The strength has to meet the load to be carried with sufficient safety and the deformation must be measured. During the test, the immediate deformation of the trusses in mid-span will be determined. This results in a relationship between deformation and load.

In the long term, deformation will increase to as much as 2.5 times this immediate deformation. This increasing deformation results from the joints, not from the nature of bamboo as a material.

Failure means a splitting of the bamboo. However, when the load has been removed, the bamboo will regain its original form. This means that a bamboo structure can survive an earthquake or storm, and that damage can be repaired temporarily by securing the split bamboo with circular lashes. The building can stay in use until a proper repair can be carried out by replacing the damaged bamboos. This is a great advantage of bamboo.

Stability

Collapse of a structure can occur not only as a result of insufficient strength, but also because of a loss of stability. This means that the structure is being loaded in a way which creates forces that the construction is unable to take. Each design has to be checked for instability. Two examples are given here, but in fact a thorough knowledge of structural design is required.

Trusses can take forces in their own plane, but for forces perpendicular to their plane (such as wind blowing against the end gable of the building) extra bracing between trusses is necessary.

41

In the lower member of a truss, tensile forces normally occur because the load acts downward. But wind can act upwards, and if the uplift of the wind is more than the weight of the roof, the lower member of the truss will be under compression force. This will result in buckling and collapse of the roof. The bracing has to prevent this.

This topic is outside the scope of this book, so only this warning is given here. Any handbook on structural design gives the full story.

Purlins

The strength of the purlins is determined by the load of a man sitting on a purlin during the erection of the building. This means that the minimum sizes for purlins are as shown in Table 3.

All the purlins have to be lashed tightly to the trusses; wind suction is a tremendous upward force!

Table 3 Ratio of size requirements

Distance of trusses	Outside diameter	Wall thickness
2m	80mm	7mm
3m	90mm	8mm

Wind

Wind load is a problem, mainly of suction: this is an upward force, by which the roof can be removed from the building.

The dead load of the roof might prevent this as long as the dead load exceeds the suction. Galvanized corrugated roof sheets are lightweight sheets, and a wind velocity as low as 20m/s is sufficient for an equilibrium between dead load and wind suction.

With fibre-cement roof sheets, this break-even point is 27 m/s. In practice higher wind speeds will occur, but with proper lashing and details bamboo trusses can survive higher wind velocity.

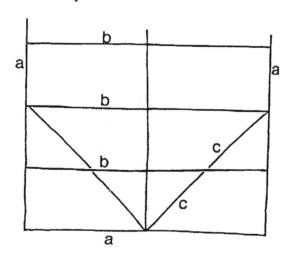

Figure 8.12: The plan of a roof

a. Building
b. Truss
c. Brace in roof (between or under the purlins; this also supports the centre of the gable wall)

Next, the danger of wind can be minimized as shown in the following diagrams. Figure 8.12 shows a plan of the roof, with stabilizing braces. Figure 8.13 shows a ridge ventilator, to control both high temperature under the roof and wind suction. Figure 8.14 shows the most dangerous situation during a storm: large openings towards the wind. To counter this, Figure 8.15 shows how to achieve suction force inside the building by creating an opening in an area away from the windward wall. If this is done carefully during a storm, taking into account changing wind directions, occupants can deliberately control the internal pressure, and save the building.

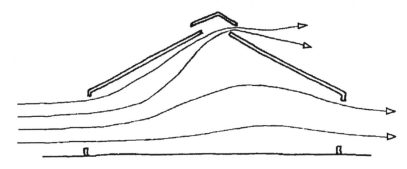

Fig 8.13: Roof with ridge ventilation

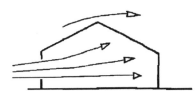

Fig 8.14: Building being blown upwards by the wind

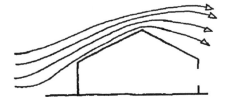

Figure 8.15: Building with suction during wind: safe

9. Bridges

In this chapter the subject will be limited to footbridges and bridges for light vehicles; excluded are bridges for heavy vehicles, floating bridges and hanging bridges. Each of them has shown its usefulness in particular cases, but for a handbook like this the area to be covered has to be limited. Some information on soil reinforcement will also be given.

Construction

Footbridge A

This bridge is shown in Figure 9.1. It is a good type for rivers with muddy or sandy bottoms, where the height of the bridge above the bed need not be more than 5 metres. The bridge is made entirely of bamboo, and the bindings are of bamboo strips.

The binding method is to make a turn with a bamboo strip round the two bamboos to be bound together, then pull as tight as possible, twist the two ends together and tuck them under the round turn. With a little practice this can be very quick and results in a secure binding. The choice between this binding and the twisted bamboo lashings depends on the normal practice of the local population. The time of construction when the bamboo is near the site is about four hours for 20 people bridging a 20-metre stream.

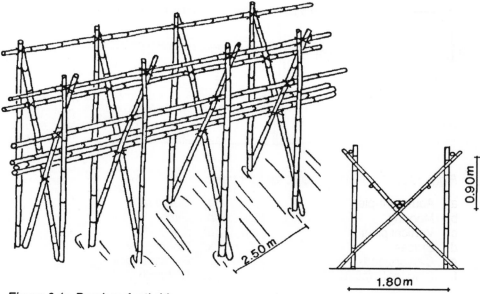

Figure 9.1: Bamboo footbridge

44

Bamboo bridge B

This bridge, for light traffic, is shown in Figure 9.2. Its components are an abutment-pier at each end, sheet pilings 3 metres apart, and a roadway.

Abutment-pier Each pier (a) is made up of two moorings (b) placed about 80cm apart. Each mooring is made of two bamboos fixed together side by side and fixed to the ground by stakes planted in front and behind.

Sheet piling The sections are placed 3 metres apart. Each section is made up of four vertical piles, of two braces (struts), of a cap (hood) and of two diagonal braces (see the cross-section).

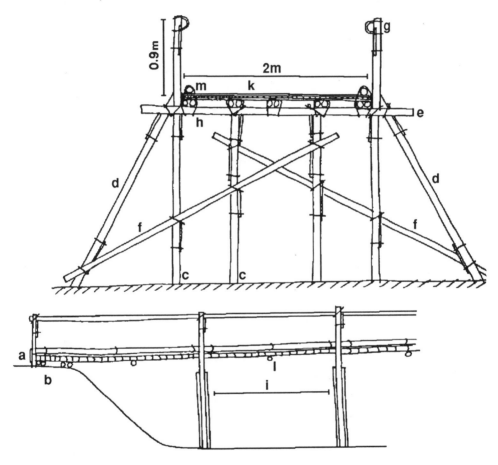

Figure 9.2: Bamboo bridge B, for light traffic

a. Abutment-pier
b. Mooring
c. Vertical piles
d. Braces
e. Cap or hood
f. Diagonal braces
g. Guard-rail
h. Girder
i. Bay
k. Flooring
l. Extra bamboo
m. Ribband

45

The vertical piles and the braces are made of bamboos of 8 to 12cm diameter at the large end. The small ends are cut back to the required length and they are cut slantwise. The piles are driven in with a sledgehammer.

The cap (hood) is made of two bamboos tied together and fixed horizontally to the piles by lashings as indicated in the detail. Two diagonal braces placed on each side of the sheet piling are also lashed to the piles.

The spacing of the piles is, in general, 75cm axis to axis. In this particular case the bamboos making the vertical piles at each end are kept longer so that the part which projects above the bridge can be used to make a guard-rail. The spacing between the two middle piles is greater than the spacing between the middle and end piles.

Bays and roadway Each girder is made of two bamboos lashed together, each with an average diameter of 10cm. Each bay is formed of five equidistant girders lashed to the caps of the sheetpiles. The flooring (surface roadway) is made of sheets of bamboo lashed to the girders. These bamboos are simply separated by the thickness of the binding (lashing) material, and they are then covered over with split bamboo. In the middle of each bay a bamboo (1) lashed crosswise to the girders distributes the stress and acts as a reinforcement device.

The ribband (m) is made of bamboos longitudinally placed on the roadway and attached to the top of the end girders to which they are secured by torsion lashing.

Maximum loads This bridge can carry 500kg per metre length. It allows both for the crossing of herds, and for either animal-drawn or open wagons with four people plus loads.

Note In this design all lashings are tightened by twisting with a stick.

Bamboo bridge C

This is a simpler version of bridge B. The *abutment-pier* is constructed of a single mooring similar to those of bridge B.

Sheet piling The sections are spaced 3 metres apart. Each section is made of two vertical piles, two struts (braces) and a cap (hood) arranged as in Figure 9.3. The piles and the braces are made of bamboos with an average diameter of 10cm at the wide end.

Bays and roadway The girders are of bamboos with an average diameter of 10cm, cut back to the required length. Each bay is made of three equidistant girders, lashed to the caps of the sheet pilings. The flooring and the ribband are similar to those of bridge B.

Maximum loads This bridge can carry 200kg per metre length. It allows the passage of people carrying merchandise on the back or on small handcarts.

Bamboo bridge D

This bridge has been designed for narrow (say 4 metres wide) and deep rivers. The design is based on flying-buttress frames.

Abutment-pier The abutment is similar to that of the other bridges.

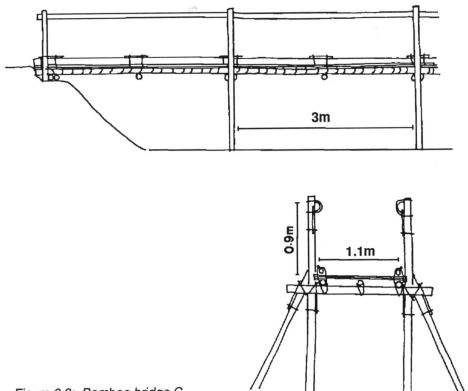

Figure 9.3: Bamboo bridge C

Frames The frames are made of bamboos of 10 to 12cm diameter at the wide end, placed and lashed as in Figure 9.4. The buttressing is consolidated by means of diagonal braces.

Roadway A bamboo acting as cap is lashed to the framework where the bamboos cross. The girders may be made either of bamboos running the total length of the bridge, or of bamboos cut back to the length which separates the cap from the moorings.

Three rows of equidistant girders are positioned as shown in the cross-section. The lashings, the ribband and reinforcement device are like those used for the preceding bridges.

Maximum loads This bridge can be used for the same purposes as the preceding bridge.

Soil reinforcement

Bamboo can be used successfully for the reinforcement of weak soil, for example, to avoid landslides or to strengthen a road. The durability is a major concern: bamboo is a natural material, and biological decay is evident if such a material is covered with soil. Under the phreatic level bamboo can live a long time, but otherwise it will decay very quickly. Chemical preservation is not appropriate because the preservatives will be leached out by the water in the soil.

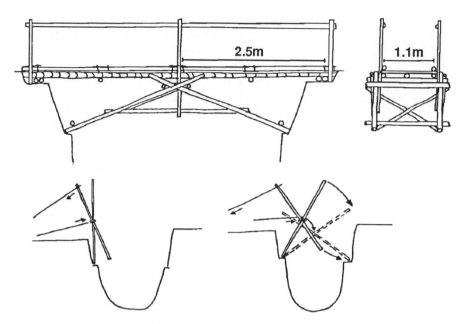

Figure 9.4: Bamboo bridge D, with flying buttressed frames, showing how to put into place (push and pull with two extra bamboos tied to the frame)

Termite attack is another problem. It is said, however, that bamboo as reinforcement under a road is not likely to be attacked by termites, because of the lack of oxygen and the vibrations caused by the traffic.

To reinforce a road, it is advisable to use a woven mat of split bamboos at intervals of 0.3 to 0.5m in both directions. This mat is placed about 0.5m under road level.

To reinforce a slope, first imagine how a failure will develop. Figure 9.5 shows a sliding plane and the collapse. The reinforcing bamboos have to prevent the sliding movement, as shown in Figure 9.5. They are laid in layers, with about 0.5m between the bamboos and 1m between the layers.

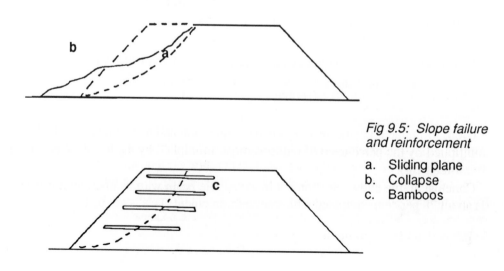

Fig 9.5: Slope failure and reinforcement

a. Sliding plane
b. Collapse
c. Bamboos

10. Concrete reinforcement

Bamboo as a reinforcement in concrete has some advantages but more disadvantages, as will be explained shortly. These can be overcome, but quite some effort is required. This means that the structural design is basically wrong, and that the designer should look into a different method such as using arches and vaults of material like brickwork or dried soil instead of beams and floors of reinforced concrete. Despite these reservations, bamboo as a reinforcement will be dealt with now in detail.

Bamboo as a cheap reinforcement

Bamboo as a reinforcement of concrete has an advantage over steel reinforcement in that steel is expensive and often requires foreign currency, whereas bamboo is cheap and is often a local material.

In concrete, the common tensile stress in steel is 160N/mm^2, and in bamboo 20N/mm^2, a ratio of 8:1. The mass per unit volume is 7850 and 500kg/m^3 respectively, a ratio of 16:1. Consequently, bamboo will be cheaper because the price by weight of bamboo will be less than half that of steel.

Bending moment

A second point to consider is the allowable bending moment in a beam with a cross-section 'b h'.

We will compare a steel and a bamboo reinforced concrete beam:

Steel reinforcement, concrete cracked, stress in steel 160N/mm^2.

$$M = 0.9h \times 0.6 \, \frac{bh}{100} \times 140 = 0.76bh^2$$

Bamboo reinforcement, concrete cracked, stress in bamboo 20 N/mm^2.

$$M = 0.75h \times 4 \, \frac{bh}{100} \times 20 = 0.60bh^2$$

(Both formulae read: distance between compression and tensile forces in the beam, multiplied by the percentage of reinforcement, multiplied by the tensile stress in the reinforcement).

Conclusion: the allowable moment in a concrete beam with bamboo reinforcement is about 78 per cent compared with steel reinforcement. This is not bad.

The width of the cracks

The stress in a steel reinforcement is 7 times that in bamboo, and the Young's modulus of steel is 10 times that of bamboo.

Consequently the strain in a beam with bamboo reinforcement is about 1.5 times that with steel reinforcement (the strain is the elongation per length).

With steel, the strain is 0.67×10^{-3}, and with bamboo it is 1×10^{-3}.

Deformation

For a concrete beam with steel reinforcement, the deformation is 1/1000 of the span, while for a beam with bamboo reinforcement this is between 1/1000 and 1/500.

The bond between bamboo and concrete

In the case of steel reinforcement, this problem does not exist. The dimensions of steel reinforcement rods can be considered to be constant, but concrete shrinks. This shrinkage causes a kind of pre-stressing to the concrete around the steel bars and, as a result, a bond between the steel and the concrete.

In the case of bamboo, however, the bamboo will normally shrink more than the concrete and no bond will result. The shrinkage of bamboo is caused by drying. When fresh concrete is poured, its water will moisten the bamboo; then, during the next month, the concrete will harden and lose water so that the bamboo will again dry out. This drying process can result in a shrinkage of the bamboo exceeding four times that of the concrete. Clearly, this drying process will completely break any bond between the bamboo and the concrete. Four possible solutions are as follows.

Technique 1 consists of melting bitumen and applying it to the bamboo strips uniformly with a brush to form a thin coat; while still hot, the bamboo is covered with coarse sand for 24 hours. The bitumen has proved an effective moisture barrier and the sand makes a very rough surface thus improving the bond.

Technique 2 uses the bitumen, as before, but 25mm nails are driven into the bamboo strips 75mm apart, so that they protrude on either side of the strip. These nails will maintain the bond.

Technique 3 again uses a bitumen coat, but the bond is provided by roughly 3mm diameter coconut fibre ropes wound around the strips at a 100mm pitch along their length. The rope is also dipped in hot bitumen before being wound around the bamboo strips.

Technique 4 uses only the outer half of the bamboo because it has a better tensile strength and a better Young's modulus, due to its higher cellulose content. The quality of the inner half is much lower by comparison. Furthermore, the outer shrinks less than the inner part. The bamboo can be split into halves and the outer used as reinforcement while the inner can be used for other purposes or just thrown away. The split bamboo halves are 10mm wide, or slightly more, and 3 to 7mm thick.

Three of these split bamboos are then twisted around each other, and the resulting cable is used as a reinforcing bar. Compared with normal bamboo, the twisted bamboo has improved characteristics.

Durability

The life of bamboo in concrete is rather uncertain. Concrete is very alkaline (the pH is 13), and this is too high for bamboo; more precisely, alkalinity destroys the pectin which sticks its cellulose fibres together biologically. Consequently, after a year or so, split bamboo changes into a mass of loose cellulose fibres because cohesion is lost. Dr H. Gram discovered this after tests at Stockholm University. Fibre-cement in which there were composite bamboo fibres of about 1mm diameter, as opposed to split bamboo with a cross-section of around 4×10mm, were tested.

It may be that the results obtained by Dr Gram are valid only for fibres, and not for split bamboo reinforcement in concrete. Until now, no work on this particular problem has been published. Sometimes an author may mention the effective lifetime of a bamboo-reinforced structure; for example, in the proceedings of a symposium, D. Krishnamurthy stated: 'Observations were carried out for over a decade and no visible signs of cracking or any damage have been noticed so far.'

This sounds satisfactory, but it is not known whether the safety factor has decreased from say, 1.7 to 1.4 and would eventually reach 1.01. Readers may think this is being pessimistic, but architects must be responsible for the structures they design and build.

Recommendation

The practice of using melted bitumen is strongly recommended, both to increase the bond (together with coarse sand, nails, coconut fibre rope, or twisted bamboos) and to protect the bamboo from alkaline attack. With these precautions, a concrete beam with a bamboo reinforcement can be designed using the following formula:

$M = 0.6 \, bh^2$

where

M = the bending moment

b = the width of the beam

h = the height of the beam.

The bamboo reinforcement should be 4 per cent of the cross-sectional area; the deformation will then be between 1/500 and 1/1000 of the span. If the height of the beam is taken as 1/10 of the span, shear stresses can be absorbed by any good concrete, so that a special shear reinforcement becomes unnecessary.

Regarding the recommended 4 per cent bamboo reinforcement, it may be difficult to find sufficient room for this quantity of bamboo. Sometimes beams are used with a cross-section like an inverted T, the wide flange at the bottom allowing more room for the bamboo reinforcement. This allows 5 or 6 per cent of bamboo reinforcement in order to obtain better strength. Practitioners have to decide for themselves which solution should be chosen: the rectangular beam, or the inverted T. The latter certainly has more space for the reinforcement, but it will give problems regarding the design of the mould and pouring the concrete.

Finally, do not underestimate the problems you will meet in trying to find space for a 4 per cent bamboo reinforcement! Remember the coarseness of the gravel in the concrete: this has to pass between the bamboos. Usually it is good practice to use only 1 or 2 per cent reinforcement, with $M = 0.15bh^2$ or $0.30bh^2$ respectively.

Once more, the reader should not underestimate the problems with shrinkage and durability. Remember also the recommendation to look into the possibilities of arches and vaults of brickwork or dried soil. Indigenous architecture in several countries shows good examples of this approach.

11. Woven bamboo

This subject deserves its own chapter, because the production is simple and moreover the market is very promising.

The production is simple, but before going into details we have to take into account a difference in fibre structure between Asian and Latin American bamboos. In Asian bamboos the fibres run perfectly parallel, which allows splitting to be done easily. In Latin America the structure of bamboo is different, and consequently splitting is difficult too. Sawing is the usual solution.

Regarding Asian bamboos, in Japan and Taiwan machinery has been developed to process bamboo, and these machines can be seen in many factories. They are very good for splitting, width sizing and other processing, but weaving has to be done manually. Weaving machines are expensive and complicated.

However, in most cases a sharp knife will do the job as well. With such a knife any villager can make split bamboo strips of around 20mm wide and 1 or 2mm thick. In Africa the author has seen a man making strips of 2mm wide and 1mm thick, and 4 metres long, with only a small knife. The result was perfect.

With a quantity of such strips, villagers can make woven bamboo baskets and other commodities. In India village populations making split bamboos and weaving them into panels of 1.2 by 2.4m are able to earn an income in the time they cannot work on their land. The production of panels of, say, 0.6 by 1.2m or 1 by 2m has potential for ceilings, partition walls, floor covers, and external walls. For these purposes the edges can be finished by bordering them, or by glueing the bamboo at the edge to all other bamboos, or by nailing the edge on to a lath.

The labour required for this woven bamboo depends on the size of the split bamboos and on the number of crossings in the woven bamboo.

In Latin America bamboos cannot be split so easily; sawing is the way to deal with bamboos here. This results in bamboo laths of about 30mm wide and 4 to 6mm thick. These are not woven but laid crosswise one on top of the other, in layers, with glue in between.

In all cases the product can be used in house construction, which helps villagers in a process of self-help building, but the product can also be finished in a more luxurious way, in order to be sold as an alternative for plywood, to be used for furniture, ceilings and partition walls in expensive housing, and for export. Feasibility studies have shown that the prices for this 'plybamboo' can compete with prices for plywood.

Figures 11.1, 11.2 and 11.3 show possible weaving patterns; the book *Bambu* by Hidalgo Lopez (see References and sources of further information) gives many more patterns.

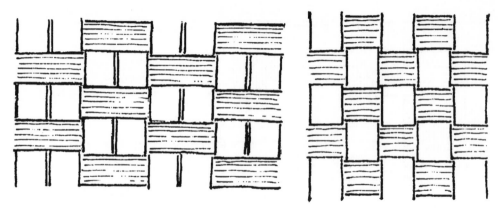

Figure 11.1: Simple weaving pattern

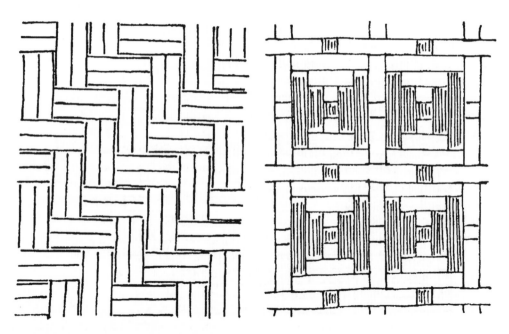

Figure 11.2: Other weaving patterns

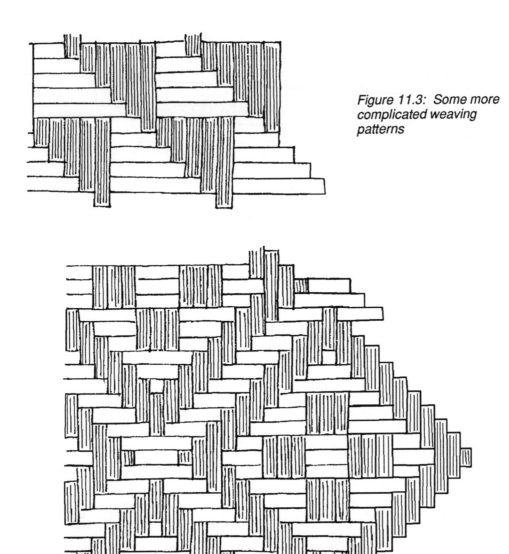

Figure 11.3: Some more complicated weaving patterns

Finally, the photographs show plybamboo production in India: the villagers in the process of splitting bamboos and weaving mats, and the resulting bamboo mats. In the evening, villagers bring these mats to the co-operatively owned factory, which basically consists of a furnace, supplying steam for the heat and the pressure needed for the glueing. The second photograph shows two bamboo mats with an intermediate layer of cheap wood; these three layers will be glued together. The final photograph shows the resulting sheets, ready for sale.

Villagers weaving mats

Bamboo mats with intermediate layer of wood

Bamboo/wood sheets glued, ready for sale

Case study — Construction of bamboo houses in Costa Rica

Introduction

The Costa Rican National Bamboo Project (CRNBP) was initiated in 1987 to address the acute shortage of housing for the rural low income population in that country. It is run under the auspices of the United Nations Development Program (UNDP) and the Center for Human Settlements (HABITAT); and the Costa Rican Government through the Ministry of Housing and Human Settlements.

The broader objectives of the Project are not only to provide low cost housing, but at the same time to set up productive employment, based on local resources, without damaging the environment. In this way, it is hoped that the bamboo housing project will promote economic and social development, and decrease both unemployment and underemployment.

It has been funded jointly by the Government of the Netherlands and UNDP. Furthermore, CRNBP has generated its own funds totalling US$1,600,000 through the construction of houses for poorer people under the Costa Rican Government's housing bonus scheme. In 1994 the project planned to generate a further US$1,400,000 for the building of new bamboo houses through the government housing programme. CRNBP has also obtained a US$4,000,000 loan from the Central American Bank for Economic Integration (CABEI), mainly to increase the number of bamboo plantations and to build several prototype bamboo houses.

The nature of the problem

The CRNBP addressed itself specifically to the rural housing shortage, as this is an area of acute need not being directly addressed by the Government housing programmes. These have tended to concentrate on the provision of urban housing, and such houses as have been built in rural areas have tended to be financially beyond the reach of the poorest people.

Furthermore, the Government programmes have concentrated on building houses of 'traditional' construction which use a great deal of wood, accelerating the deforestation process and further degrading the rural environment.

Scope of the project

The pilot stage of the CRNBP began in 1988 and was completed in 1991. Its aim was to tackle the problems outlined above as well as using participative processes of dialogue and consultation to build prototype rural houses more suitable to the inhabitants' needs, and provide much-needed work for whole families; women and young people as well as men. The lightness of bamboo makes it particularly suitable for use by all family members.

In doing so, the Project also aimed to build houses comfortable enough to make it more likely that peasants and small farmers will want to stay in the rural areas to earn their livings and not be so readily attracted to the urban centres. In this respect the productive activities element of the bamboo project was of key importance.

To build such houses, CRNBP has utilized technologies it has developed making use of bamboo *(mainly guadua spp.)*, cana brava *(gynerium spp.)*, and wood.

Communal organization

It has been possible to give in-service training to the new householders regarding 'self help' construction methods, so that whole families have built together, not just learning about house construction methods but the importance of communal organization and the benefits of mutual help. Each family has been involved not just in building their own house, but those of their neighbours too.

After the conclusion of each housing project, the people involved felt highly motivated and stimulated to achieve other goals, including the improvement of aqueducts, electrification, as well as building churches, meeting centres and sport facilities.

In this first phase of the project, the conditions were right for people to become quickly involved in various activities including the extraction and preservation of bamboo, the fabrication of bamboo panels for house building, and to begin the programme of house building itself. So it was that families were able not just to solve their immediate problem of inadequate roofing/housing, but to learn techniques and skills that will enable them to earn a living and generally improve their quality of life.

At the beginning of the project it was decided to cultivate as many bamboo plantations as possible in order to replace wood – which is becoming ever more costly and scarce – in significant quantities. At the time of writing, it is estimated that with the production of *guadua* for the next year, it will be possible to build 3,000 dwellings per year on a sustained basis. This quantity represents about 15 per cent of the total number of houses that the country must build in order to meet housing targets by the year 2000.

As well as providing a natural, renewable, low cost construction material, bamboo plantations make an important contribution to the effort to halt the rampant felling of the remaining natural forest on the island and the destruction of the rich biological diversity they contain.

Achievements

Plantations

It was decided to plant the *guadua* species of bamboo because of its suitability for construction work. It is long and straight, with a good grain and high strength. The two forms of *guadua*, 'Sur' and 'Atlantico' were found to be the most successful in tests on propagation, fertilization, thinning and establishing nursery areas. Thus healthy plantations were propagated very rapidly.

In three years it was possible to obtain 85,000 bamboo plants, from which 65,000 were used to plant 179 hectares distributed throughout the country. Some of the remaining plants were exported to neighbouring countries attempting to establish bamboo plantations.

Construction
During the pilot stage 296 dwellings were built in rural and semi-urban areas of the country, including 92 houses in three different Indian communities located within the Boruca Terraba Indian reserve.

Research and development
A research and development centre was established alongside the construction department to deal with drying and preservation and to address any problems that might arise. It also carries out research into improved techniques and practices and methods of quality control.

Preservation
A problem which emerged early in the project was insect (*Dinoderus*) attack on pieces of bamboo in use. A low-cost preservative was successfully tried, together with some simple techniques to preserve bamboo culms, and boards and laths made from split bamboos.

Treatment is carried out to combat *Dinoderus*, termites and other insects using boron compounds. These are low-cost, easy to obtain and of low toxicity for human beings. Also, they can be easily recycled. For the treatment of culms, a modified form of the Boucherie method (see pages 9-10) is used. For the treatment of esterillas and reglillas (narrow boards or laths made from bamboo, used in house building and furniture making), a dip (as opposed to soaking) diffusion method is used.

Insect attack is now not a problem provided these techniques are used.

Structural design
Considerable attention has been paid to the physical and mechanical properties of bamboo when used as a construction material, particularly its performance in earthquake conditions.

The resultant designs and techniques were given a real test in 1990 when more than fifty CRNBP houses were shaken by the earthquakes of Cobano, Puriscal and most of all Limon, which measured 7.6 on the Richter scale. Thirty of the houses withstood the earthquake without any damage.

As part of the same research programme, designs were developed for a special type of bamboo structure, consisting of twenty bamboo poles of the same length and six identical metal joints, enabling large roof spans such as those required in meeting centres, sports halls or churches to be successfully constructed in bamboo.

Other products
It is envisaged that the CRNBP is approaching the point where there are sufficient quantities of bamboo grown in its own plantations to satisfy the housing demand

identified at the outset. Research has therefore begun into additional, economically viable uses for bamboo. One such use is furniture making. A three-year programme has resulted in successful prototypes of chairs, tables and beds being made in serial production, appropriate machinery being developed and several people being trained to manufacture the furniture.

Production of plybamboo, particleboard and fibreboard have also been considered. Those products can replace tropical hardwoods and plywood in the internal construction market, and feasibility studies suggest that there are good possibilities for export.

Training

Considering that *guadua* was a completely new plant, never before used as a construction material in Costa Rica, the process of technical training in bamboo construction techniques was a priority set by the pilot stage of the CRNBP. At the end of that stage (1991) it was very satisfying to know that the successful training of many people in bamboo utilization had been accomplished, including 400 family members as well as about 60 technicians, trained specifically in bamboo planting and plantation maintenence, preservation and drying; the construction of dwellings and furniture making; as well as in communal organization and directing small-scale rural enterprises.

Conclusions and follow-up activities

The first stage of the Costa Rican National Bamboo Project has been successful owing to its firm foundation on the principle of sustainability, and because the bamboo construction system developed by CRNBP has been demonstrated to be reliable, durable, earthquake-resistant and much more economical than the traditional construction systems.

Very often, the relatively high investment needed to undertake projects concerned with small-scale sustainable development, such as the CRNBP, is felt to be unaffordable by many governments in developing countries. This is despite the fact that such projects can have substantial environmental, social and economic benefits in the long term.

Yet the CRNBP has achieved a great deal with a relatively small amount of national and external funds, which have been used to provide equipment for training, technology transfer and research and monitoring activities.

Because of this success at relatively low cost, there is much international interest in the CRNBP, particularly in other Central American countries.

References and sources of further information

References

In writing this book the author has used not only his own experience, but also much information exchanged with colleagues in past years. He wishes to thank them all. Some authors have been referred to more explicitly and are listed here.

Gram, 'Durability of natural fibres in concrete', Ph.D. Thesis, Stockholm, 1983.

Hidalgo Lopez, Oscar, *Bambú, su cultivo y aplicaciones*, Estudios Tecnicos Colombianos Limitada, Colombia, 1974 (Spanish), 318pp.

Kirkpatrick and Simmonds, 'Bamboo borers and the moon', in *Tropical Agriculture*, vol.35 no.4, Trinidad, October 1958, pp.299-301.

Krishnamurthy, D., *Use of Vegetable Plants and fibres as building materials*, Proceedings joint symposium Rilem/CIB/WCCL, Baghdad, October 1986, pp.C71-C78.

Royal Engineers, *Training Memorandum*, No. 17, 1945, p.57 (Bridge A).

Trojani, F. *Bulletin Economique IndoChine*, April 1930, (Bridges B, C and D).

Note Hidalgo Lopez's book is available from: PO Box 50085, Bogota, Colombia. This is a very good handbook, covering all subjects: cultivation, paper industry, physical and mechanical properties, preservation, reinforcement in concrete, buildings, bridges, water pipes, woven bamboo. Many good drawings and pictures.

Further reading

Arce, O., *Fundamentals of the design of bamboo structures*, Doctoral thesis, Eindhoven 1993, 261pp. ISBN 90-6814-524-X.
   The handbook for engineers. Deals with the mechanical behaviour of bamboo, and joints, and the design of structures.

Austin, R. and Ueda, K., *Bamboo*, Weather Hill, New York, Tokyo, 1972, 216pp. ISBN 0-8348-0048-9.
   Wonderful pictures, with a good text. Not for the field practitioner; more specifically for those who like attractive books, and bamboo.

Dunkelberg, Klaus, *Bambus als Baustoff*, Rudof Habelt Verlag, Bonn, 1980, 286pp. Am Buchenhang 1, 53 Bonn 1, Germany. 1985 edition edited by Institute for Lightweight Structures, University of Stuttgart, Germany.
   This book is an excellent report on bamboo housing in Asia. The author gives many drawings and pictures made during his own travels. Unfortunately both editions are out of print.

Farrelly, David, *The Book of Bamboo*, San Francisco, 1984, 340pp. ISBN: 0-87156-825-x. Sierra Club Books, 530 Bush Street, San Francisco, CA 94108.
Describes anything that possibly can be done with bamboo, but at a newspaper level.

Hidalgo Lopez, Oscar, *Nuevos Tecnicos de Construcción con Bambú*, Estudios Tecnicos Colombianos Limitada, Colombia, 1978, (in Spanish), 137pp.
Contents: low-cost housing, soil-cement plaster on a split bamboo base as roofing material, bamboo-reinforced cement and concrete for water containers, flat panels, beams.

Janssen, J.J.A., *Bamboo in Building Structures*, Doctoral thesis (Eindhoven, 1981) 235pp.
Describes the mechanical properties of bamboo, and joints and trusses.

Janssen, J.J.A., *Mechanical properties of bamboo*, Kluwer Academic Publishers, Dordrecht-Boston-London, 1991.
Tables on the mechanical properties of bamboo. For engineers only. Available from: Dr J.J.A. Janssen, University of Technology, PO Box 513, 5600 MB Eindhoven, The Netherlands.

Janssen, J.J.A., *Bamboo trusses*, Eindhoven, 1983
A manual on how to build trusses. Many pictures and scarcely any text, in English. Just for the field practitioner, 65pp. Available from the author.

Janssen, J.J.A., 'Bamboo: Its use in the construction of roofs and bridges', *Appropriate Technology*, vol. 10 no. 2, September 1983, pp. 20-23.

Liese, W., *Bamboos: Biology, silvivs, properties, utilization*, GTZ, PB 5180, D 6236 Eschborn 1, Germany, 132pp. ISBN 3-88085-273-1.
This books gives a very good overview of the mentioned subjects. It is a must for everybody.

Ranjan, M.P. et al, *Bamboo and cane crafts of Northeast India*, National Institute of Design, Paldi, Ahmedabad 380 007, India, 1986, 344pp.
Gives many good and clear drawings and examples.

Villegas, M., *Tropical bamboo*, Rizzoli Int., New York, 1990, 175pp. Translated from: Bambusa Guadua, Bogota 1989.
A very good book on building and handicraft in Colombia. Many colour photographs.

The World of Bamboo, Heian Int. Inc., San Francisco, 1983, 236pp. ISBN: 0-89346-203-9., PO Box 2402, South San Francisco, CA 94080, USA.
Expensive book, but marvellous colour photographs.

Termites

Dancy, H.K., *A Manual of Building Construction*, IT Publications, London, 1975, pp.68-74.

Søe, Thorkil, *Stop Termite Attack on Buildings*, Erla Publishers, Svenstrup, Denmark, 1982, 54pp.

Mossberg, B., *Termites and construction*, Lund Centre for Habitat Studies, 1990, 22pp. From: Lund University, Box 118, S 221 00 Lund, Sweden.

Machines to process bamboo can be purchased from:

- o Takahashi Bamboo and Rattan Machinery Works Ltd, Nomura Building, 1-1, 2-chome, Ohtemachi, Chiyoda-ku, Tokyo 100, Japan

- o Chin Yung Machine Works, PO Box 52, Lukang, Taiwan

Both have good catalogues (free on request).

Bamboo Information Centres

- o India: Bamboo Information Centre, India.
  Kerala Forest Research Institute,
  Peechi, 680 653, Trichur, Kerala, India.
  Publishes the *BIC India Bulletin.*

- o China: Bamboo Information Centre,
  Chinese Academy of Forestry,
  Wan Shou Shan 100 091,
  Beijing, China.
  Publishes *Bamboo Abstracts.*

- o Latin America:
  c/o Proyecto Nacional de Bambú,
  Apartado 21-1350,
  San Sebastian, San José,
  Costa Rica.

The first two are fully operational, the third is a newcomer and is in Spanish.